BULLDOG
MADNESS

GOLDEN AGES
OF COLLEGE SPORTS

BULLDOG MADNESS

Great Eras in Georgia Football

WILTON SHARPE

CUMBERLAND HOUSE
NASHVILLE, TENNESSEE

Published by
Cumberland House Publishing, Inc.
431 Harding Industrial Drive
Nashville, TN 37211-3160

Cover design: Gore Studio, Inc.
Text design: John Mitchell

Library of Congress Cataloging-in-Publication Data

Sharpe, Wilton.
  Bulldog madness : great eras in Georgia football / Wilton Sharpe.
      p. cm. — (Golden ages of college sports)
  Includes bibliographical references and index.
  ISBN 1-58182-447-5 (pbk. : alk. paper)
  1. Georgia Bulldogs (Football team)—History. 2. University of Georgia—
Football—History. I. Title. II. Series.
  GV958.G42S43 2005
  796.332'63'0975818–dc22

                                                              2005011396

Printed in the United States of America
1 2 3 4 5 6 7—10 09 08 07 06 05

*For Charley Trippi and Francis Tarkenton,
when it meant something to be a
college football hero,
and
for Caroline,
whose devotion to our love is as vast and
encompassing as her dislike for sports in general,
though she really liked Athens*

Charley Trippi

CONTENTS

INTRODUCTION

The distinguished gray-haired gentleman sitting opposite me on the aisle of the bus rifled quickly through the five football playing cards of himself that had been handed to him to look at.

"Yes," said 74-year-old Charley Trippi, "I've seen all these."

"No you haven't," interjected his wife, Peggy, politely correcting the former University of Georgia and Chicago Cardinals star running back. "You've never seen this one."

It was Friday night, August 15, 1997. The bus, waiting patiently in the parking lot of Sportsman's Park race track for other members of the 1947 NFL champion Chicago Cardinals to board, would soon escort the players to yet another function celebrating the team's 50th anniversary reunion.

I had interviewed the great Trippi for a magazine article on that wondrous '47 team only months earlier. Now I had the chance to meet the legend, my collection of Trippi trading cards offering the perfect conversational entrée. I had been well aware of Trippi's Pro Football Hall of Fame credentials garnered over nine seasons in the NFL, but not until I began researching this book did

I become aware of his brilliant and electrifying career forged in Athens.

And Trippi, as well as those before him, was only the tip of the Bulldog iceberg.

Star after star was unveiled, from Sinkwich to Sapp, from Trippi to Tarkenton, from Walker to Greene; the great teams under W. A. Cunningham, Kid Woodruff, Harry Mehre, Wally Butts, Vince Dooley, and Mark Richt; the storied rivalries with Auburn, Florida, and Georgia Tech; the multitude of great moments—Sinkwich in the 1942 Orange Bowl, Trippi in the '43 Rose Bowl, Buck Belue to Lindsay Scott, Herschel Walker's superhuman three-year reign over college football.

On these pages, the story of Georgia Bulldog football unfolds through quotes from the great Georgia players and coaches, opponents, members of the media, and even from the fans themselves.

If you've ever yelled, "How 'bout them Dawgs!" or wished you could've pulled on a pair of silver britches, *Bulldog Madness* is for you.

It's all Dawg.

— W. S.

REMEMBRANCE

The dormitory room in the western Massachusetts school was conspicuous for its unabashed display of idolatry. Thumb-tacked to the walls was an august gallery of gridiron heroes, carefully culled from the annuals and sports magazines of the era.

My favorites were clustered galaxy-like on and around a smallish bulletin board suspended over the study desk. The occasional color photo brightened the array of mostly black and whites—those old posed stances that all players were photographed in before the era of high-speed film and higher shutter speeds. All were inspirational, especially those of the quick-cutting backs and high-leaping passers. A few were less motivating, particularly those showing the ends standing on the ground holding a ball at the tip of their extended arms.

One special favorite was of a quarterback posed in a passing stance, slightly elevated off the ground, silver helmet gleaming. The caption read: "Francis Tarkenton, Georgia quarterback." Of course anybody knowledgeable of The Scrambler's career knows that the media referred to him as Francis, not Fran, while at Georgia.

Filling my head with more visions than sugarplums at Christmastime, the Bulldog field general regularly leapt from the photo wall into my realm of fantasy, the images working their magic, infiltrating to the degree that I almost seemed to take osmosis-like cues from Sir Francis when out on the football field. Like my hero, I also wore No. 10.

A quirky side effect of idolatry is that it can unexpectedly fuel the occasional good performance. I became a starter at quarterback my junior year. In the season opener, against a school from Avon, Connecticut, all was going well. We were up, 20–0, and by early in the fourth quarter victory was assured. That's when my concentration began to wander. As frivolous daydreams persist in the interminable stretches of classroom ennui, so now images of the sleek Georgia quarterback, frozen in wondrous posture on the photo wall, shelled me like flack on the playing field.

I called for a Y–In, a pass to the right end on a slant-in. With unscripted embellishment, I took two steps down the line then leaped high in the air, back arched, arm cocked mightily behind my head, left arm jutting straight to the skies. The preposterous scene telegraphed to the defense that a jump pass was on its way to the single receiver coming out from the right side, a pass that was effortlessly intercepted. As I trotted back to the sideline, head bowed, the coach bellowed for all to hear, "What were you, posing for the cover of *Sports Illustrated?*"

Embarrassed beyond all sufferable allowance, I found little room to hide on the bench. Mercifully, time soon ran out, the shutout preserved. Walking to the locker room, it was difficult to ignore the profundity of this latest piece of education: Posed shots in magazines don't necessarily reenact well in game conditions on the field. Be a player, not a poser.

For that afternoon at least, the Georgia Peach was safe from a daydreaming pretender gaining on him from the ranks of the wannabes.

— W. S.

BULLDOG
MADNESS

ORIGINS:
EARLY INKLINGS
OF RED

D r. Herty simply tossed the football in the air and watched us scramble for it. He selected the strongest-looking specimens for the first team. Luckily, I was the one who recovered the ball, and thus I was assigned a position.

George Shackelford
UGA letterman (1893),
in the fall of 1891

BETWEEN THE HEDGES

Georgia football was fathered by university chemistry professor Dr. Charles Herty in 1891. As a graduate student at Johns Hopkins, Herty had witnessed the maverick rugby-style sport firsthand.

Within days of his return to Athens, Herty paced off the first football field in UGA history, on a student play area located in a quadrangle between several campus buildings. According to author Charles E. Martin, it was "hardly more than an ash dump, with practically no grass and covered with clinkers and pebbles."

Reportedly Herty, carrying a copy of Walter Camp's football rulebook, walked onto the field and gathered some students around him for a brief instructional session. Several days after laying out that first gridiron on the Athens campus, the field was named for Dr. Herty.

L ong before three o'clock the crowd began to assemble and the yells of the two colleges were alternately raised with a vim by the boys. The university goat was driven across the field by the boys and raised quite a ripple of laughter.

John F. Stegeman
author,
on the Georgia–Mercer game, January 30, 1892,
the first football game in UGA history

S hackelford grabbed a Mercer back and pushed him back of his own goal, making safety.

Athens Banner
February 2, 1892

I picked up the ball carrier and slung him over one shoulder, carrying him (football and all) 20 yards back across his own goal line.

George Shackelford
at age 70, recalling the abovementioned safety
in the Georgia–Mercer game

GEORGIA WINS
FIRST-EVER GAME

Prior to Dr. Charles Herty's return to Athens in the fall of 1891, no collegiate football had been played south of Raleigh, North Carolina. Shortly after laying out Herty Field, Dr. Herty scheduled Mercer for Georgia's inaugural football game.

The contest, played on January 30, 1892, was a whitewash, as Georgia hammered out a convincing 50–0 win.

Reported the Athens Banner *in its February 2 edition: "The Mercer boys brought two (train) cars full of students and citizens. . . . Macon colors, black and yellow, were seen on nearly 200 breasts . . . a nicer crowd never came on a visit to Athens. Enthusiasm was supreme. When the game ended, the boys were riding around on a sea of shoulders. Even the goat was ridden."*

The University boys make with their yells a music unheard since the old Confederate yell died in our land.

Athens Banner
on the train ride to Atlanta for the inaugural Auburn–Georgia game in 1892

At the Kimball House tickets for the game went fast at 50 cents for adults, 25 for children. Carriage spaces sold for a dollar. Signs announced that the best way to Piedmont Park grandstand was by way of the Peachtree Street horse-cars or by the Edgewood Avenue electrics. "Every tally-ho, dray, T-cart, surrey, dos-a-do and conveyance that can be found in the city" was reserved for the game.

John F. Stegeman
on the 1892 Auburn–Georgia pre-game atmosphere

UGA, AUBURN INITIATE SOUTH'S LONGEST RIVALRY

Georgia and Auburn clashed for the first time at old Piedmont Park in Atlanta, inaugurating the Deep South's longest football rivalry.

The contest, scheduled for February 20, 1892, was the Red and Black's second game in their inaugural season.

Dr. Herty had contacted a former class-mate at Johns Hopkins, Dr. George Petrie, then of the Auburn University history department, and arranged a game between the two schools.

The Red and Black's elevated spirits following the shellacking of Mercer turned to disappointment, however, when the Alabamians took home a 10–0 win.

Reports of the day indicated that the billy goat, Georgia's pre-bulldog mascot of the time, was the main course in a Georgia bar-becue held after the game.

The dye from our red caps had run and had turned our long hair into a bright vermillion. Our faces were streaked with a hue that contrasted biliously with the red clay.

A. O. Halsey
Bulldog letterman (1892),
in the wet, solemn aftermath of Georgia's
10–0 loss to Auburn

His excellent work has been seen constantly. He has built up the team wonderfully in the short time he has been with us.

Athens Daily correspondent
in 1896,
on early UGA head coach "Pop" Warner

FAST FACT: *Glenn S. "Pop" Warner, the first big-name head coach in Athens, later became a legend for coaching stints at Carlisle, where he coached the legendary Jim Thorpe, and at Stanford, where he tutored football's all-time ironman, Ernie Nevers. During his brief two years at UGA, Warner distinguished himself, becoming the first head coach to take the Red and Black through an undefeated season. In 1896, Georgia went 4–0 against Wofford (26–0), North Carolina (24–16), future national powerhouse Sewanee (26–0), and Auburn (12–6).*

GEORGIA FIGURES IN
FIRST FORWARD PASS

In Pop Warner's second game as Georgia head coach, in 1895, against North Carolina, an unprecedented play took place. Oddly, it was allowed to stand, paving the way for a North Carolina victory. The fallout from the play, however, would be a harbinger of the most potent offensive weapon in the history of the sport—the forward pass.

Backed up near his own goal line, the Carolina punter, pressed to get his kick off in the face of a heated Georgia rush, inexplicably flung the ball far downfield. A startled teammate caught it and "was running through all obstructions like lightning and had touched the ground back of the Georgia goal," according to one report.

Since the forward pass was not listed in the rules of the day, mayhem ensued. But an official failed to rule against it, claiming he "didn't see it." The following day, the pass was called a "clever trick" in the Atlanta Journal's *account.*

A decade later, esteemed coach John Heisman, a spectator at that Georgia–North Carolina game, wrote to Walter Camp proposing that the forward pass be legally adopted to open up the game. In 1906, it was.

Von Gammon is a promising youth. He is but 16 years old and a freshman but he punts like a veteran.

Harry Hodgson
Atlanta Constitution, *October 11, 1896*

He was the star of the Georgia team— Von Gammon.

Bill Stern
legendary 1940s–'50s sportscaster

Grant me the right to request that my boy's death should not be used to defeat the most cherished object of his life.

Von Gammon's mother
*in a letter to Georgia Governor Atkinson
after her son's death resulted in a state legislative
attempt to ban football at Georgia, in 1898.
As a consequence of Mrs. Gammon's letter,
Atkinson vetoed the bill and the sport
was spared*

VON GAMMON DEATH
STIRS FOOTBALL BAN

October 31, 1897. A day of infamy in the history of University of Georgia athletics. Sophomore star fullback/linebacker Von Gammon was killed in a game against Virginia.

Gammon's death touched off a powder keg of backlash against the sport. Overnight a ban on football at all schools receiving state funds was called for by the state legislature.

The bill only awaited the signature of Georgia Governor W. Y. Atkinson to become law. But then Gammon's mother made an impassioned plea in a letter to Atkinson.

"It would be the greatest favor to the family of Von Gammon," she wrote, "if your influence could prevent his death from being used as an argument detrimental to the athletic cause. It would be inexpressibly sad to have the cause he held so dear injured by his sacrifice."

Atkinson deferred to the request and never signed the bill.

The young star's death was not in vain. A national outcry resulting from additional football-related deaths ultimately prompted President Theodore Roosevelt to demand more safety for the sport.

We would have been run off the field by any freshman team of today. We knew nothing of conditioning, had no training table, and ate anywhere and anything we pleased. Compare our old dressing room in the basement of Old College with the dozens of training rooms in the Coliseum today. We wore the same uniform for practice as in the games and toward the end of the season we were a disreputable sight. No two uniforms looked alike.

Hugh Gordon
left tackle (1900),
in 1965

THE MCWHORTER YEARS—
UGA'S FIRST ALL-AMERICAN

Georgia's first powerhouse era, under Coach Alex Cunningham, also produced its first-ever All-American—halfback Bob McWhorter.

McWhorter, a local Athens product, starred from the time he entered UGA as a freshman, in 1910. In each of his four seasons he was named All-Southern.

In his final year, as captain of the Red and Black, he was selected to renowned New York Herald *sports journalist/author Parke Davis's 1913 All-America Team, the first Southern player ever to be so honored.*

Georgia closed out the four-year McWhorter era with a total of 25 wins, six losses, and three ties. At UGA, McWhorter scored 63 touchdowns.

CUNNINGHAM'S INFAMOUS "WATER BOY PLAY"

During and following the McWhorter era, Coach Cunningham concocted a successful scoring play that would be considered ludicrous today.

With no NCAA by-laws to police college football's early days, unusual plays surfaced, usually exiting overnight as new rules outlawed them. Such was Cunningham's "Water Boy Play."

A "sleeper" player basically hid out along the sidelines, dressed in white overalls and carrying a bucket as the water boy. At the snap, he would throw down his pale and dash downfield to receive a pass, usually wide open with no one near him.

Georgia used the trick play in a game against Alabama. Fans rioted on the field afterward, but since no uniform dress code existed then, the play was allowed to stand.

T hus ended the first quarter-century of the intercollegiate game in the Deep South. Twenty-five years before, Charles Herty had thrown out a football on Georgia's campus field, and told the boys to scramble for it. George Shackelford, who came up with the ball, became the first of the University's gridiron immortals whose spirits, in the imagination of many an old-timer, still hover above old Herty Field. Shackelford, Nalley, Ketron, Moore, Woodruff, Hodgson, McWhorter, Paddock . . . all are names that will live in campus lore as long as there is a football to pierce the autumn air.

John F. Stegeman

TRADITION

I f you can't appreciate the swaggering gait and Churchillian physiognomy of Uga V, the Bulldogs' bulldog, you must be a cat lover.

Sports Illustrated
April 28, 1997

BETWEEN THE HEDGES

Only the passage of time has a way of writing the most appropriate text on tradition. But loyal Georgia fans brush up against UGA hallowedness every time they don their red and black on fall Saturdays. From the Georgia media guide:

"The Georgia tradition is 'Between the Hedges' and 'How 'Bout Them Dogs.' It's 'Silver Britches' and 'Let the Big Dog Eat.' It's college football's most celebrated mascot, 'Uga.' It's playing in the country's fifth-largest on-campus stadium before more than 92,746 of the Bulldog nation."

It's also new and young student-athletes following the greats of the game—Sinkwich, Trippi, Tarkenton, Stanfill, Walker, Woerner, Hoage, Hampton, Hearst, and Pollack. Here are a few more takes on Bulldog tradition.

The tradition and great players who have gone to Georgia over the years have always impressed me. When you step onto that field with your teammates, the electricity in the air is amazing and having the chance to be a part of that will last a lifetime.

Eric Zeier
quarterback (1991–94; captain, 1993–94)

Larry Munson is a homer. He is for Georgia. There is bias in his voice, and it is there on purpose. Still, I know officials of other schools who have walked up to him and said, "I wish you called our games. You're the best I've ever heard."

Loran Smith
Lewis Grizzard
authors,
on the longtime Bulldog radio announcer

Where a player comes from, how he spells his name or his nationality, does not matter . . . just as long as he is proud of that red jersey and tries like hell to score for the University of Georgia.

Wally Butts
head coach (1939–60)

UGA's first president, Abraham Baldwin, was a Yale graduate, and the first buildings on the Georgia campus were based on blueprints from Yale. The tenacity of Georgia's teams, plus the strong ties with the Eli, resulted in the emergence of the nickname "Bulldogs" in 1920.

Derek Smith
author

T he "Georgia Bulldogs" would sound good because there is a certain dignity about a bulldog, as well as ferocity.

Morgan Blake
Atlanta Journal, *Nov. 3, 1920*

FAST FACT: Three days following Blake's article, Georgia fought Virginia to a scoreless tie. In the game account, the Atlanta Constitution's *Cliff Cheatley repeatedly referred to Georgia as the "Bulldogs." The name has stuck ever since.*

A thens is ablaze with enthusiasm tonight. Students and citizens alike are painting the town red and black.

Atlanta Constitution
after Georgia's first-ever victory over Auburn, November 24, 1894—a 10–8 win in Atlanta

E AT 'EM GEORGIA

Badge worn by UGA rooters in 1901

to the Auburn–Georgia game in Atlanta. Pictured on the badge was a bulldog tearing a piece of cloth—the first-ever mention of the animal that 20 years later would begin its longtime run as UGA's mascot

T he demonstration here tonight is unprecedented in the history of the institution. . . . The chapel bell has been kept ringing.

Atlanta Constitution

following the scoreless tie with heavy favorite Auburn in 1901. The bell has tolled for Georgia victories ever since. Students take turns tugging the rope into the wee Sunday morning hours

I t's gonna be sad not having the Track People there. When the team drives up on the buses for the game, and we see all of them, and know some of 'em stayed all night up there, you get both chills and a warm feeling at the same time.

Scott Woerner

cornerback/punt returner (1977–80)

FAST FACT: *The "Track People" were a hearty breed of the Georgia faithful and a staple of UGA tradition since 1929, the year Sanford Stadium first opened. The Tracksters would perch precariously atop the railroad tracks overlooking the east end of the stadium and wildly root the Bulldogs on. But construction enclosing the east end in 1980 brought to an end this adventurous and colorful UGA supporter.*

G eorgia pride is a very special feeling.

Vince Dooley

head coach (1964–88)

Before the 1980 season, Vince Dooley decided the Bulldogs would revert to the silver pants worn during Wally Butts's tenure. The pants and the cry "Go you silver britches!" became trademarks of the campaign, as they had been during Butts's regime.

Derek Smith

An *Atlanta Journal* reporter, apparently unfamiliar with "Glory, Glory to Old Georgia," complained of the incessant playing of "John Brown's Body."

John F. Stegeman

detailing an account from the November 10, 1906, Georgia–Georgia Tech game in Athens. The UGA fight song, "Glory, Glory," sung to the tune of "The Battle Hymn of the Republic," is one of the oldest traditions at Georgia and has been rendered at games since the 1890s

The famous English privet hedges that surround Sanford Stadium's playing field were only one-foot high when the stadium was dedicated in 1929 and were protected by a wooden fence. It was natural for a clever sportswriter, referring to an upcoming home game, to observe "that the Bulldogs will have their opponent 'between the hedges.'" At least one old-timer says the phrase was first coined by legendary Atlanta sportswriter Grantland Rice.

**University of Georgia
media guide**

It meant something special to me to put on that red jersey. While I had speed, I was still pretty small. But when I put on the red jersey, I felt big and strong.

Kent Lawrence
tailback (1966–68)

THE RED
AND BLACK

If I had really had a bad disposition throughout my career, I could have done a lot of things.

Bill Stanfill

defensive tackle (1966–68, captain 1968),
Outland Trophy winner (1968),
All-America (1968)

BETWEEN THE HEDGES

The roll call starts with two Heisman Trophy winners and a Maxwell Award recipient who tallied more first-place votes for the Heisman than the winner did in 1946.

First-team All-SEC selections (including the All-Southern picks before that) number in excess of 250. More than 60 Bulldogs swell the ranks of Georgia's first-team All-Americans.

McWhorter, Woodruff, Catfish Smith, Hartman, Sinkwich, Trippi, Rauch, Sapp, Dye, Tarkenton, Walden, Patton, Chandler, Stanfill, Scott, Robinson, Woerner, Walker, Belue, Hoage, Butler, Worley, Hearst, Zeier, Ward, Stinchcomb, Bailey, Greene, Pollack . . . the names still hum with the wonder of their deeds.

Woodruff of Georgia! When might and strength failed to find an opening and the way seemed blocked, a curly blonde head upon a lithe and agile body would bob through, wriggling, twisting, dodging.

Grantland Rice
Atlanta Journal,
on Georgia's star quarterback
(1907–08, 1910–12)

Quarterbacks may come and quarterbacks may go, but I would rather see that little bunch of nerve leading my team than any man I have ever seen.

Alex Cunningham
head coach (1910–19),
on Kid Woodruff's announcement that he
would return for the 1911 season

S tudents who watched the practices in the fall of 1910, or who just happened to take a peek out of their dormitory windows, beheld the astonishing sight of a thick-legged freshman running wild from one end of Herty Field to the other. This was Bob McWhorter. . . . He ran, with a deceptive, changing stride, that made it almost impossible for a single man to bring him down. Usually it took at least three.

John F. Stegeman

FAST FACT: McWhorter scored an even 100 points in his freshman season.

T o Northern enthusiasts, McWhorter comes as a stranger. But not so in the South, where he is known as the most phenomenal backfield player the game has known in years.

Parke H. Davis
writer/author who selected McWhorter to his 1913 All-America Team, the first player ever selected from the South

If there's a football player we've had who was maybe as good or better than Herschel Walker, it's Bob McWhorter. They were built along the same lines, and they ran practically the same way, and they were fast. Bob McWhorter was a great athlete.

Buck Cheves
quarterback (1919–20)

He ran time after time, never tiring, calling the signals, doing the punting, backing up the line, engineering the trick plays, shooting the forward passes. Aside from this, he was of no use to Georgia.

Atlanta Constitution
*on 1914 Georgia All-America quarterback
Dave Paddock*

You won't see ends block any better than George Poschner did it. He knocked them out of there.

Wally Butts

I didn't play with a headgear, and I didn't get hurt—but I think I'm suffering for it now. Artie Pew wouldn't wear one either. I expect Artie and I were the only two, and he's dead and I'm half dead.

Buck Cheves
at age 82

Charley Trippi's superior value was on defense. For sure tackling, I never saw his equal among backfield men. After Trippi, you had Charlie Britt, Buck Bradberry, Claude Hipps, Andy Dudish, Art DeCarlo. They were some folks who would really hit you.

Wally Butts

Lamar "Racehorse" Davis averaged 28 yards per catch in 1942, and you can hardly beat that. For consistency Van Davis was the best in 1941 and 1942. Jimmy Orr, George Poschner, Harry Babcock, Johnny Carson, and a lot of others were great, but Lamar Davis was the best receiver.

Wally Butts

Van Davis stymied virtually every attempt the Bruins made to circle his end. The celebrated Bob Waterfield sneak didn't fool Van and his sidekicks, Red Boyd and Bulldog Williams. They were waiting for that one and it just wouldn't work.

Paul Zimmerman

author/writer,
on the 1943 Rose Bowl 9–0 victory over UCLA

John Rauch was a custom-built football player. Coach Butts made him a quarterback during the summer of 1945. They spent the entire summer practicing the art of quarterbacking, and I understand Rauch took his laundry by the railroad station several times, but he did not go home. He stuck it out and became a precision quarterback, intelligent and fearless. He was the most precise quarterback I have seen.

Bill Hartman
*fullback (1935–37, captain 1937),
assistant coach (1939–42, 1946–56, 1974–94)*

The best signal caller? It would be mighty close between Francis Tarkenton, Cliff Kimsey, and John Rauch. All three were great at carrying out a plan.

Wally Butts

AP/WIDE WORLD PHOTO

John Rauch

onsidering the quality of teams he played on during his career at Georgia, Zeke Bratkowski is undoubtedly one of the greatest players in the school's history. . . . Bratkowski ended his career in Athens as the school's all-time leader in passing and total offense (his 4,863 yards total offense was not surpassed until 1982 when Herschel Walker moved into the number one spot with 5,259 yards).

George Scherer
author

FAST FACT: *Bratkowski, a three-time Associated Press All-SEC second-team quarterback, played at Georgia from 1951 to 1953 and captained the '53 squad.*

Z eke Bratkowski was the best mechanical passer, but we had several fine ones. John Rauch, Heyward Allen, Trippi, Tarkenton, and Jim Todd. If I had to pick just one, Rauch would be the man.

Wally Butts

L ook at Fran Tarkenton, who played at Georgia and then set numerous career records in the National Football League. Fran got by on desire, determination, brains, cunning, guile, quarterback arrogance, and quickness.

Vince Dooley

F ran Tarkenton and Pat Dye were leaders and fine football players. On the field Tarkenton was a great leader, and he read the defenses better than any quarterback we ever had.

Wally Butts

B obby Walden and Zeke Bratkowski both led the nation, and you can't get much higher. Pat Field, Cliff Kimsey, and Charley Trippi were also outstanding punters.

Wally Butts

He has the best potential of any place-kicker we have ever had. Right now Durward Pennington is in the class of Leo Costa, Pat Jernigan, Joe Geri, and Bobby Walston.

Wally Butts

One of our 1964 quarterbacks, Preston Ridlehuber, had excellent running ability. He was strong and ran with speed.

Vince Dooley

When Don Shula reached a peak with his great Miami Dolphins teams in the seventies, who were his stars on defense? Jake Scott and Bill Stanfill, members of that great recruiting class at Georgia in 1965.

Vince Dooley

We never had a more effective option runner than Ray Goff. He appeared slow because of his size, but he was really pretty fast. He was a swivel-hipped runner with the great leg strength.

Vince Dooley
on the quarterback and captain of the
1976 SEC champs

I 've never seen an athlete with his positive attitude as a punt returner. It's tough to catch a football in punting situations because if you make a mistake, everybody in the house knows you have failed. That kind of pressure never bothered Scott Woerner. He enjoys it.

Bill Lewis
assistant coach (1980–88)

B enjamin Franklin Belue. But you don't call a kid Benjamin Franklin down in South Georgia. Ben would have worked, of course. Even Frank. But how about Buck? That's perfect. There are sports names, and then there are sports names. Buck Belue. I've heard few better.

Loran Smith

He's got ice water in his veins. He looks at you with that cold stare, and he never tips you off to what he's thinking.

Wayne McDuffie
*assistant coach (1977–81, 1991–95),
on Buck Belue*

If you come to Georgia, others will follow.

Wayne McDuffie
*to young Valdosta prospect Buck Belue,
in 1977. Until Herschel Walker arrived,
no Georgia recruit ever received more attention*

When it came to the big play, no defensive player we ever had could match Terry Hoage's overall ability and performance, even though he was not the great natural athlete. Jake Scott made many great plays, but he was the natural athlete. Terry was an over-achiever if there ever was one. His play-action timing was extraordinary. There has never been a smarter defender to wear the Red and Black.

Vince Dooley

Defensive back Tony Flack is the only player we ever recruited who started the first game of his first year. Not even Herschel Walker and Lindsay Scott started in their first games.

Vince Dooley

FAST FACT: Flack played from 1982 to 1985.

E ric Zeier is not just a real good quarter-back, he's a force. He's a real leader and competitor and he knows his position. He may be the best quarterback I've ever seen. He's as good as I've ever competed against.

Bill Curry
former Georgia Tech, Alabama,
and Kentucky head coach

AP/WIDE WORLD PHOTO

Eric Zeier

H e's the best. He's the best quarterback in Georgia history, the best quarterback on any campus, the best passer this conference has ever seen. Talk all you want about Namath and Manning and Sullivan and Spurrier and Parilli, but none ever threw so often so well. If Eric Zeier misses a receiver . . . you catch yourself feeling a bit deflated, as if you'd seen Lord Olivier trip over the floodlights.

Mark Bradley
Atlanta Constitution

C hamp Bailey had the potential to dominate either side of the ball in any game. In his final season at Georgia, Bailey won the Bronko Nagurski Award as college football's top defensive player and ranked among the nation's best wide receivers with three 100-yard games and more than 750 yards overall.

Mark Vancil

editor

Champ Bailey

A lot of what he does simply doesn't show up on a stat sheet, but when every coach leaves the stadium, he knows Champ Bailey had as much of an impact on the outcome of the game as anyone.

Greg Williams
assistant coach (1996–98)

Former offensive lineman Matt Stinchcomb and cornerback Champ Bailey were Georgia's lone representatives on the SEC's 1990 All-Decade Football Team first-team announced by the league. Running back Garrison Hearst was named to the second-team.

Anthony Dasher
Morris News Service

In Georgia's regular-season finale, on November 27, 2004, a 19–13 win over Georgia Tech, David Greene passed Peyton Manning to become the Southeastern Conference's leader in career passing yards. The four-year starter has thrown for 11,264 yards. Three weeks earlier, Greene broke Manning's record for Division I-A wins in a 62–7 victory over Kentucky. Manning, now the Indianapolis Colts' quarterback, won 39 games at Tennessee from 1994–1997.

ESPN.com

He's a leader. Things don't get done unless he starts them, and he is the commander of an army. He keeps everyone calm during tight situations.

Fred Gibson
wide receiver (2001–04),
on David Greene

He's extremely accurate. He threw the ball right on target. Forty wins for him . . . that's hard to do in a college career.

Rich Brooks
Kentucky head coach,
on David Greene

David Greene

If I could hope, maybe it would be just the guy that found a way to win. Not for being the best quarterback, but one who found a way.

David Greene

quarterback (2001–04),
on how he would like to be remembered
at Georgia

FAST FACT: *Greene, the winningest quarterback in NCAA Division I-A history, posted a 42–10 record as a four-year Bulldog starter.*

We thought he'd be a starter someday and do some good things, but we never dreamed he'd do the things he's done.

Mark Richt

head coach (2001–),
on three-time All-America defensive end
David Pollack

FAST FACT: *Pollack, winner of the 2004 Lombardi Award (nation's top college lineman) and 2004 Bednarik Award (nation's best defensive player), is the first Georgia player to win either award.*

I would not have predicted David Pollack to be the player of the year in the league, but I knew whoever had to play against him down after down would have a long day because of how hard he plays and how long he can play hard.

Mark Richt

*on Pollack's brilliant 2002
sophomore campaign*

He was solid. He's a guy that you want to know where he is.

Barry Alvarez

*Wisconsin head coach,
after Pollack's 2005 Outback Bowl
MVP performance against the Badgers*

AP/WIDE WORLD PHOTO

David Pollack

P laying a new position at the start of his sophomore season in 2002, David Pollack was anything but an unknown by season's end, setting a school record with 14 QB sacks which also led the SEC. He was named one of five finalists for the Bronko Nagurski Award (nation's top defensive player) and was voted the SEC Player of the Year by league coaches and SEC Defensive Player of the Year by the Associated Press. The 2002 Bulldogs defense finished first in the SEC and led Georgia to the SEC and Nokia Sugar Bowl championships and a final national ranking of No. 3.

georgiadogs.com

BULLDOG CHARACTER

An awesome attitude is best described as a "bad case of the wants."

Erk Russell
legendary Georgia defensive coordinator
(1964–80)

I'm the luckiest guy in the world to be alive.

George Poschner

*tight end (1940–42),
after the Bulldogs' 9–0 Rose Bowl victory
over UCLA in 1943*

I'm still the luckiest guy in the world to be alive.

George Poschner

*from Walter Reed Hospital,
Washington, D.C., in 1947,
after surviving a bullet through the head
and losing both arms and legs in World War II's
infamous Battle of the Bulge*

I never met a braver football player.

Bill Stern

on George Poschner

I believe that the people who make it in the world aren't the most talented ones or the smartest or the luckiest, or necessarily the bravest. The ones who make it are the dogged ones. Just plain tenacity; the ones who take the jolts and get up and look at the sky. And no matter what's there, they'll say, "Well, I've got to do it; so let's go." The athletes have an expression for it—suck it up. Other people do the same thing, in their own fashion. And whether they realize it or not, that's the real serenity of living; coping in some civil, meaningful, and positive way with the problems that come.

Francis Tarkenton
quarterback (1958–60, captain 1960),
private credo, tacked to his business office wall

I see something in the game that is very valuable. I realize it is not fashionable to speak in favor of football, but I have watched it ever since it came to Georgia and I have formed opinions about it. First, more men are saved by the training than are injured by the game. . . . Then it has, to a large extent, stopped fighting [among the students] and is the best training in self-control that I know of.

Chancellor David Barrow

*the first UGA president to publicly
endorse football, 1905*

Football is the most democratic game in the world. It makes no difference where you come from, what your race or religion is; there's only one way to become a good football player: That's through hard work and ability. There are no short cuts. You have to pay the price to be good.

Wally Butts

Down Georgia way a one-armed football player—Ed Barrett—caught four forward passes and intercepted three others during one game in October 1930. Little football boy had a busy day!

Bill Stern

I n his junior season, Frank Sinkwich ran and passed South Carolina to death in a game as brutal as any old-timers can remember. A knee caught him in the jaw and broke it. The Georgia trainer devised a protective mask that covered half of Sinkwich's face, and his picture appeared across the country wearing his jaw guard. Two weeks later, in New York City against Columbia, Georgia won the game and Sinkwich won the press, the jaw protector having as much to do with spreading his fame as his play.

Furman Bisher
longtime sports editor,
Atlanta Journal-Constitution

My father impressed upon me at an early age that a commitment is a commitment. "Be a man of your word," he always taught me. "Do what you say you are going to do." And it was my mother who always said, "Manners will take you where money won't."

Vince Dooley

After modestly accepting his awards, he was not heard to mention them again in public. He was never sure that excelling in sports was a great accomplishment in itself. For him athletics were pleasurable and wholesome diversions that complemented the more serious phases of college life.

John Stegeman
on Georgia's first All-America selection,
halfback Bob McWhorter

FAST FACT: In 1954, McWhorter was elected to the College Football Hall of Fame.

I don't believe there is any better oppor-
tunity than to have the chance to
become a Georgia Bulldog. The Georgia
program makes you respect yourself both
as an athlete and as a student. It makes you
believe in yourself.

Herschel Walker
tailback (1980–82),
1982 Heisman Trophy winner,
three-time consensus All-America
(1980, '81, '82)

I just try to take things one day at a time and whatever happens, happens.

Rodney Hampton

tailback (1987–89, offensive captain 1989)

If it is to be, it is up to me.

Lanice "Chuck" Jones

wide receiver (1980–82)

I have a certain philosophy about life. I think you should work two-thirds of your life to enjoy the last third, and that's what I'm doing right now.

Charley Trippi
at age 59

A way back yonder, when I was starting out to squire the girls, my father told me: "Son, don't sit around after you've run out of something to say. Pick a time when you're both laughing. Then get your hat and leave."

Vince Dooley
*on announcing his retirement after 25 years
as Georgia's head coach*

LEGENDARY
COACHES

I t was as if a dormant volcano had suddenly blown its top, spitting fire for the next 22 years.

John Stegeman
*on the naming of assistant coach Wally Butts
as Georgia head coach in 1939*

BETWEEN THE HEDGES

The names Butts and Dooley readily come to mind, but a memorable parade of other colorful and talented mentors have manned the Georgia sidelines.

• **GLENN S. "POP" WARNER**, *one of the legendary icons in college football history, began his head coaching career in Athens in 1895, guiding the Red and Black to its first undefeated season in 1896.*
• **ALEX CUNNINGHAM** *(1910–1916, 1919) produced winning records seven of his eight years at Georgia.*
• **HERMAN J. STEGEMAN** *led UGA to its first Southern Conference championship, in 1920.*
• **GEORGE "KID" WOODRUFF**, *an outstanding quarterback in the McWhorter era, brought the Bulldogs their first national championship with the Dream and Wonder Team of 1927.*
• **HARRY MEHRE** *(1928–37) boosted Georgia's national prominence, defeating Yale five straight times when the Ivy League school was at its height, the only university in the country to do so.*

G rantland Rice once observed that it would be difficult to determine whether Pop Warner or Knute Rockne had the greatest overall effect on the game of college football.

Richard Whittingham
author/sports historian

Y ou cannot play two kinds of football at once, dirty and good.

Pop Warner
head coach (1895–96)

I really wasn't a very good recruiter. Oh, I went after the boys all right, but I couldn't demean myself. I couldn't soft-soap a kid and his family to get him to sign when I knew I'd be chewing him out six months later.

Harry Mehre

They are saying in New York tonight that Harry Mehre is one of the great young coaches in football.

Ralph McGill
Atlanta Constitution,
after Georgia's 7–6 victory over NYU at the Polo Grounds in New York, November 8, 1930

I tell people I had a lifetime contract at Georgia and that the school got out of it by declaring me legally dead.

Harry Mehre

If a lineman missed a block in practice, Butts would put him back there with a ball in his hand like a quarterback and let somebody run over him. "That's how the quarterback feels when you miss your block," he'd tell them.

Charley Trippi
halfback (1942, 1945–46, captain 1946)

Butts would have been good even if he had been a preacher. That's what preachers make you do—believe. He could make you believe.

Charley Trippi

Coach Butts was really far ahead of his time in his approach to football tactics. He was a pugnacious little guy who could talk like a carny worker on the practice field and lead us in prayer the next day.

Francis Tarkenton

We pray before our games, too, but I've noticed God always seems to be on the side of the team with the biggest and fastest players.

Chuck Mills

former Wake Forest head coach

Wallace Butts has proven once again that he is the greatest football coach in America.

Frank Leahy
Notre Dame coaching legend,
after Butts's undefeated 1946 season

Anyone who watched Georgia during the Butts years can remember the "temper tantrums" he threw on the sidelines when something happened to upset him. He'd begin by waving his short, stubby arms like he was about to take flight, then he would appear to throw some imaginary object to the ground. The fit would end as he swung his right foot forward as if to kick the offending image out of sight.

George Scherer

There are no more loyal players anywhere than those who are loyal to Wallace Butts.

Vince Dooley

The guy who really got me ready psychologically and technically for college football was Quinton Lumpkin, the freshman coach at Georgia. He had been a great center at Georgia (1936–38, captain 1938) and was the kind who lived in the dormitory with the players—a principled, hard-fibered, decent guy who was a man among men. Nobody ever challenged Quinton Lumpkin. He was tough, all right, but a gentle guy at the core, a man you could confide in if things got rough. We played three freshman games and won them all (1957), and two weeks before the varsity's opening game, we beat the varsity.

Francis Tarkenton

When you talk about kicking, you talk about Bill Hartman when you come from Georgia. He's really the first person who led me down the right road to kicking, who made me pick up the fundamentals and turn what seems like a physical sport into a mental game. That's what Coach Hartman did best. He created a good feeling when I went out on the field.

Kevin Butler
kicker (1981–84; special teams captain 1984)

This was a team of country boys from Georgia, and Coach Whit spoke our language.

Francis Tarkenton
on assistant coach J. B. Whitworth
(1939–49, 1959)

FAST FACT: *After a 10-year absence from Coach Wally Butts's staff, Whitworth returned as an integral part of the 1959 SEC champion Bulldogs.*

oach Butts greatly influenced the coaching career and philosophy of Shug Jordan, who influenced mine.

Vince Dooley

FAST FACT: Dooley was an assistant coach under Jordan at Auburn from 1956–63.

told Joel Eaves (UGA athletic director) that if he was fool enough to stick out his neck for me, I was fool enough to take the job.

Vince Dooley

FAST FACT: As an Auburn assistant coach in 1963, Dooley was invited to take the head coaching job at Georgia.

don't believe the successful integration of our school systems in the South, in the late '60s and early '70s, would have ever come about as orderly as it did without athletics.

Vince Dooley

I deally, in this business you need to change jobs at least one time.

Vince Dooley

I t's work to keep your name out of the papers regarding other jobs.

Vince Dooley

I can't imagine why Dooley would even consider leaving three more years of Herschel Walker.

Georgia fan
*when the Bulldog coach was a candidate for
the Auburn head coaching vacancy after
the 1980 season*

W e've got too much invested here. All these players, all these teams. I love Georgia too much to leave.

Vince Dooley
*to his wife, Barbara, upon deciding to decline
the head coaching job at his alma mater,
Auburn, in 1980*

Erk Russell. What a coach! What an unforgettable character! What a man! He was the cornerstone of our staff for 17 years.

Vince Dooley

Early on he would butt heads with our players in pre-game warm-ups. He would enter the locker room with blood streaming down his face, and you could see the fire in his defensive players' eyes. He was going to war with them.

Vince Dooley
on Erk Russell,
Bulldog assistant coaching legend

Communication is the most important coaching technique in football. Without communication there can be no teaching, and teaching is coaching.

Erk Russell
assistant coach (1964–80)

I can't say enough about him. He's a player's coach. He inspires a ballplayer. I've probably had two pints of blood spilled on me in pre-game warm-ups where he'd butt you and hit those rings on your pads and knock that scab off his head and bleed all over you.

Bill Stanfill
on Erk Russell

The players had confidence in him and they loved him because they knew he loved them. Erk motivated through leadership and teaching, not enforcement. Yet he had the macho image. He certainly had a lot to do with the 201 victories posted by the name of Vincent Joseph Dooley.

Vince Dooley

oach Donnan is like a father figure. He gets involved with his players and makes you feel at home. He puts his players in a position to display their talents.

Champ Bailey
cornerback (1996–98, captain 1998)

s the 2001 season closed, Mark Richt had become the first Georgia coach since H. J. Stegeman in 1920 to win eight games in his inaugural season.

georgiadogs.com

He definitely has a special aura about him. He came from a program that had seen so much success, and he's got that confidence about him that draws people to follow him. I think when he first got here, he made a lot of quick believers.

Jon Stinchcomb
tackle (1999–2002),
on Mark Richt

One thing that I like so much about him is I think he has the whole football thing in perspective. He doesn't put it ahead of everything else in his life. I think that's important.

David Greene
on Mark Richt

Beats workin'.

Erk Russell
on coaching

WINNING AND LOSING

Coach, ain't they good to you when you win!

Bill Godfrey
fullback (1959–61),
to Wally Butts,
after Georgia beat Alabama, 17–3, in the
season opener, September 19, 1959

No one on this football team ever quits. You've got to win some like this to stay undefeated. And what a run Lindsay Scott made!

Vince Dooley

after Buck Belue's 93-yard scoring pass to Lindsay Scott enabled Georgia to squeeze past rival Florida 26–21, with 1:20 left, to remain undefeated during the Bulldogs' 1980 national championship season

Smiles always follow victory. They never precede battle.

Loran Smith
Lewis Grizzard

I learned early in my career that winning has a definite impact on communication. When you win everybody relates, everybody communicates. When the record is bad, the rumors abound and the perceptions become skewed to unbelievable proportions.

Vince Dooley

H e would always draw a clear picture of what was at stake. He would dramatize and clearly define what our role was in any given situation. In doing so, he made it perfectly evident to everybody on the team what we could accomplish by winning.

Chip Wisdom
linebacker (1969–71),
assistant coach (1975–80),
on Vince Dooley

I don't think we can take this every week, but we have to take them any way we can.

Quincy Carter
quarterback (1998–2000),
on UGA's 23–22 victory over LSU,
October 2, 1999, at Sanford Stadium

FAST FACT: *Bulldog linebacker Will Witherspoon's leaping deflection of Tiger quarterback Josh Booty's two-point conversion passing attempt preserved Georgia's one-point lead after LSU had scored with just 18 seconds left. Then-10th-ranked UGA held on to remain undefeated at 4–0.*

E rk Russell fought for the underdog role, and no coach has ever used that role any better. It never bothered me if the defensive players felt they were second-class citizens. It gave them a rallying point, and teams with rallying points often play winning football.

Vince Dooley

W hen you don't win enough football games, they are going to find something wrong with you and the way you coach, no matter what.

Vince Dooley

I don't think the blame is all his when we lose, but he accepts it. He does so openly, and he doesn't wait for somebody else to get around to it. Players appreciate that.

Chip Wisdom
on Vince Dooley

We don't have to win them all. We've got a sane situation here. Everybody understands we are playing a big-league schedule on a shoestring, and if we can beat Tech two times out of three and win most of the rest, we are doing well.

Harry Mehre

We should have won that game against Georgia Tech. We were upset, and we had to live with it the rest of our lives. It bothers me today. I'll never forgive, nor will I forget.

Harvey Hill
*halfback (1927–28),
member of the '27 Dream and Wonder team
that blew an undefeated season and a
Rose Bowl berth in losing the season finale
to the Yellow Jackets*

POST HASTE

On March 23, 1963, a story appeared in The Saturday Evening Post *implicating Georgia athletic director and former head coach Wally Butts and Alabama head coach and athletic director Paul "Bear" Bryant with collaborating to fix the outcome of the 1962 Georgia–Alabama game.*

The Post *took the unproven claim of insurance agent George Burnett, whose long-distance call to an Atlanta public relations firm somehow wound up being connected to the phone line on which Butts and Bryant were talking. Burnett, taking copious notes, charged that he heard Butts giving Bryant information which may have led to Alabama's 35–0 white-washing of Georgia.*

Butts was shattered by the allegations, resigning from his AD post before his libel suit against the magazine even came to trial. A federal jury found no truthful basis for the Post *story and awarded Butts $3,060,000, later reduced to $460,000. Bryant settled out of court for $300,000. The awards, huge for that time, virtually put the* Post *out of business. Still, Butts never seemed completely recovered from the devastating magnitude of the story, even though he and Bryant both were acquitted of the charges.*

Whenever you lose a game to a team that's not as good as you are, that's the coaches' fault. It happens every week.

Pat Dye
guard (1958–60, captain 1960)

We played in the Gator Bowl stadium 27 times during my years at Georgia, winning 19 and tying one. There were only three times that we were not in the game in the fourth quarter.

Vince Dooley

Our whole life was dedicated to winning. If we lost the football game we'd go back to the dormitory and provoke a fight or something to take out our frustrations. We hated losing back then. Of course, when you played for Butts, he made you hate losing.

Charley Trippi

Y ou've got to do everything well, but you've got to play defense first.

Vince Dooley

F or the past two decades, Georgia has drawn specifically from those early '80s teams as their points of pride. We just want to make that a perennial experience that comes along with the University of Georgia.

Jon Stinchcomb
2002

It's a great season. Three years in a row with 10 wins is not easy to do. Obviously, we had goals. We wanted to go undefeated but 116 other teams dream the same thing.

David Greene
concluding his record-setting career
after the 2004 campaign

They fought hard and won. We fought hard and lost.

Ralph "Shug" Jordan
legendary Auburn head coach,
after the Tigers' one-point loss to Georgia
in the 1959 SEC title game

THE GREAT GEORGIA TAILBACKS

No back ever wore the Red and Black with more success than Charley Trippi.

Jesse Outlar
sports journalist/author

BETWEEN THE HEDGES

They are legends now—Georgia's first All-American, a tailback, Bob McWhorter, who rambled unchecked through opponents from 1910 to 1913; 1942 Heisman Trophy winner "Flatfoot" Frankie Sinkwich; 1946 Maxwell Award recipient Charley Trippi; 1982 Heisman Trophy winner Herschel Walker . . . but the list doesn't end there.

Both before and after Walker, the line of dominating tailbacks wore on: Joe Geri, Kent Lawrence, Jimmy Poulos, Glynn Harrison, Kevin McLee, Willie McClendon, Lars Tate, Keith Henderson, Tim Worley, Rodney Hampton, Garrison Hearst, Terrell Davis, Robert Edwards . . .

The only other collegiate institutions rivaling Georgia's brilliance in tailback output are Southern Cal and Ohio State. But ask any of the Bulldog faithful and it's doubtful they'd trade any pigskin lugger from Athens for what Troy or Columbus might offer.

The word great is the most abused in the lexicon of sports. Almost every game, contest, or performance produces the "greatest" play or the "greatest" player in history. But when you call Frankie Sinkwich "great" you are guilty of nothing more than understatement. The Georgia back not only is great, he's colossal, terrific, magnificent, grand, glorious, and anything else you might find in the thesaurus which we consulted. The show Frankie the Fireball put on in the Orange Bowl New Year's Day definitely proved that the transplanted Ohioan is deserving of recognition as one of the best ever to play football. There never was a more brilliant individual act, and that goes for Red Grange's act against Michigan.

Sam Butz
Jacksonville Times Union, *January 2, 1942*

I have never seen a better runner in college football than Sinkwich. They knew he was coming and they loaded the dice, but he just ran over them. He also got the quickest start and had the greatest acceleration of any back I have ever seen.

Wally Butts

on 1942 Heisman Trophy winner
Frank Sinkwich

How could Georgia miss with Sinkwich, the Man in the Iron Mask, the fireball from the red clay hills of Athens?

Lamont Buchanan

author

Wild Boar Sinkwich is not only a powerful runner but a spectacular one to watch. . . . Really, customers should be charged double to see him tuck a ball under his arm and bolt like lightning into the line.

Zipp Newman

Birmingham News, *1940*

AP/WIDE WORLD PHOTO

Frank Sinkwich

Frank Sinkwich, a combination of poetry in motion and you know what on wheels, pitched passes which led to four touchdowns and sped 43 yards to a fifth score to spark the University of Georgia football team to victory. The final score of your Orange Bowl game—the wildest game ever played in any bowl any time—was 40–26, with TCU putting on an amazing finish after trailing by 33 points early in the third period. The cracked-jaw Cracker from Youngstown, Ohio, was every inch an All-American as he put on a spectacular exhibition of passing and running which left both the Horned Frogs and the cash customers breathless.

Everett Clay
Miami Herald, *January 2, 1942*

Sinkwich finished his junior year with an incredible record. For he personally outrushed the entire Mercer, South Carolina, Columbia, Alabama, Florida, Centre, Dartmouth, Georgia Tech and TCU teams. He failed to do it against only two teams—Auburn and Ole Miss. Sinkwich finished with another admirable record. He was a marked man in every game—but he was never stopped. He fumbled only one time all year. At the close of a great season he looked like one of the best passers the South has produced. He was tops as a runner. He finished as America's best back. The one or two selectors who left him off All-America must wonder about what fools some mortals be.

Jack Troy

BULLDOG MADNESS

The favorite expression on Sinkwich is that he ran into a group of people and spit them out on both sides like a lawnmower cutting grass. He held all the offensive records until Willie McClendon broke them.

Bill Hartman

"Triple threat" is an unfamiliar concept to today's football fans, weaned on the specialized modern game. Frank Sinkwich was a true embodiment of the term: He ran, he passed, and he kicked. Though just 180 pounds, he knew no fear and gained most of his yards between the tackles from the ancient single-wing formation. He also played defense, which was necessary in those one-platoon days.

Furman Bisher

Which was the better player, Sinkwich or [Charley] Trippi? That's always been a subject of debate. I think maybe Trippi isn't recognized for what he is—the best safetyman the South ever saw. He was also a great offensive football player, no question about that. Sinkwich carrying the ball, though, was just as good an offensive player as I've ever seen.

Bill Hartman

Trippi is the best football player I have ever seen. I almost got away for a touchdown today on a kickoff, but Trippi got me. I believe I could have faked anybody else. But you just don't fake Trippi.

Charlie "Choo Choo" Justice
North Carolina 1949 All-America halfback,
who played against Trippi in the
1947 Sugar Bowl

I nto Frankie Sinkwich's spot in the spotlight stepped a worthy successor: Charley Trippi, a 20-year-old sophomore, who made Georgia's victory possible by gaining 115 of their 212 yards rushing and did most of the passing. Here is a great football player. Put his name in your mind. He is as sure to blaze a trail to fame as the sun is to set.

Jack Troy
Atlanta Constitution, *January 2, 1943,*
after Trippi's MVP Rose Bowl performance

C harley Trippi was a gifted athlete. During that 1940–60 period, I never saw a better one, and I officiated and went all over the country and saw Billy Cannon and Lance Alworth—all of them.

Porter Payne
tackle (1946–49)

Charley Trippi

Charley Trippi of the University of Georgia, without question, is the greatest football player I have ever seen anywhere.

Bobby Dodd
*All-America quarterback for Tennessee in 1930,
legendary head coach at Georgia Tech*

Trippi was a great running back and one of the best safeties in the game, as well as a fine punter. He won the Maxwell Award in 1946 and was runner-up to Army's Glenn Davis for the Heisman.

Richard Whittingham

After seeing Trippi in the (1946) Oil Bowl, I went home and turned Sammy Baugh's picture to the wall.

Morris Frank
Houston newspaper columnist

I won't pick between Sinkwich and Trippi. I know I was fortunate to coach the best two backs any coach ever had on the same team.

Wally Butts

Willie McClendon was a big back with speed who could make that tough yard inside, and he could sprint to the corners on sweeps. We also used him to go over the top in critical short-yardage situations. He was an exceptional back, one of our truly great players.

Vince Dooley

J immy Poulos, "the Greek Streak" from Marietta, Georgia, had saved his best for last. He grabbed a screen pass from Andy Johnson and then weaved and twisted his way through Maryland defenders on a 62-yard touchdown that old grads compared to Charley Trippi's unforgettable 68-yard punt return against Tulsa in the 1946 Oil Bowl. It was the last touchdown the exciting Poulos would score for Georgia.

Jesse Outlar
on the UGA tailback from 1971 to '73
and his finale in Red and Black—
a 17–16 Peach Bowl victory over the
Terrapins, December 28, 1973

I n the late 1970s, collegiate scouts from Southern Cal to Ohio State were drawn to rural Wrightsville, Ga., to watch a soft-spoken youngster who wrote poetry and shredded opposing defenses as a running back at Johnson County High School. The feverish recruiting wars ended in April 1980 when Herschel Walker signed with Georgia.

Derek Smith

N ot since Frank Sinkwich and Charley Trippi in the 1940s has there been a ball carrier to excite the University of Georgia football fans the way an 18-year-old freshman, Herschel Walker, has in only two games for the Bulldogs.

New York Times
September 1980

I t looks like Walker will be changing a few defenses as he goes along.

Johnny Majors

*former University of Tennessee head coach,
on freshman Herschel Walker, named both
AP and UPI Southeast Back of the Week
after his collegiate debut in 1980, which helped
produce a come-from-behind, 16–15 opening-
game win over the Vols in Knoxville*

H ottamottiedang! Herschel's gonna be the only player in history to win the Heisman Trophy four years in a row!

Bulldog fan

*exiting Sanford Stadium after Georgia had
beaten South Carolina and George Rogers,
13–10, November 1, 1980*

AP/WIDE WORLD PHOTO

Herschel Walker

Herschel was never a fancy runner with a unique style. He had speed and power. He could stop and start. He was strength personified. He was more like a heavyweight boxer who kept coming at you. When you get into the 13th, 14th, and 15th rounds, you separate the champion from the rest. That was Herschel Walker.

Vince Dooley

He walked like a Greek god and ran with the harsh grace of a rhino.

Furman Bisher

on Herschel Walker

He was so big, I thought he was a tackle. His speed for his size is amazing.

Frank Sinkwich

*upon seeing Herschel Walker, then a
high school junior, for the first time*

H erschel Walker, a two-time All-American entering his junior year, was the nucleus of Georgia's return to national prominence in the '80s. The tailback rewrote the record book almost every time he touched the ball. Walker owned eight NCAA rushing records and needed only 15 yards against Florida in 1982 to become the NCAA's fifth all-time leading rusher. In the 44–0 whitewash of the Gators, Dooley began substituting freely and Walker was done for the day, with 219 yards and three scores.

Derek Smith

W ith Herschel it was three basic plays: Herschel right, Herschel left, Herschel up the middle.

Vince Dooley

L ars Tate was always into the game. He practiced hard, and he played hard.

Vince Dooley
on the Bulldog tailback from 1984 to '87

K eith Henderson seemed to make exceptional catches so often. Great extension to get to the ball and the ability and awareness to keep his feet in bounds. He was versatile and probably had the best instinctive awareness of any back I coached. He really had a feel for where he was on the football field. That is something you don't coach. He weaved and flowed, whereas Tim Worley was a pounder, a blaster. Worley could blast off tackle and go 75 yards with the best of them.

Vince Dooley

FAST FACT: *Henderson and Worley both played in the years 1985, '86, and '88.*

The night we played him, I'm not sure an NFL team could have stopped him.

Rockey Felker
former Mississippi State head coach,
on Tim Worley

Tim Worley is the most physical and abusing runner we've seen in a long time. . . . We needed two weeks off just to get over him.

Bill Brewer
former Ole Miss head coach

Tackling him is like being hit by a 100-car freight train loaded with cinderblock.

Unknown opposing defensive back
on Tim Worley

Georgia has its legends—Walker, Trippi, Sinkwich, Tarkenton—and mentioning anybody in the same breath with them borders on lunacy. But I suggest Rodney Hampton is rapidly approaching their status.

Billy Harper
columnist, Athens Daily
November 2, 1989

Of all the backs I've ever coached, none could stop and start as quickly as Rodney Hampton. From dead stop to top speed was only a couple of steps for him.

Vince Dooley
on the Georgia tailback from 1987 to '89

Perhaps Rodney Hampton doesn't look as fast as Herschel Walker, because he sort of glides when he runs. But try and catch him. He can motor. He reminds me of a Glynn Harrison with speed.

Billy Harper

R odney Hampton has that all-around ability that you want in an offensive back. He's a tough inside runner and has the good speed to get outside. He's a great open-field runner and has good hands. Rodney has absolutely no inhibitions about catching the ball over the middle and he knows how to block. All those things are needed to be a complete running back, and Hampton does all those things very well.

Willie McClendon

*tailback (1976–78, captain 1978),
running backs coach (1989–93)*

G lynn Harrison could change directions without slowing his speed better than any back we had at Georgia.

Vince Dooley

FAST FACT: Harrison played from 1973 to '75 and was captain of the 1975 team.

arrison Hearst is phenomenal. He has so many moves, if you blink twice, you might miss four or five of them and he'll be in the end zone.

Lynn Swann
former Pittsburgh Steelers
three-time Pro Bowl wide receiver
and current TV analyst

e's awakening the echoes of Georgia's Heisman heritage.

Chris Fowler
ESPN college football host,
on Garrison Hearst

arrison Hearst has a natural talent that only a few people in the world are blessed with, and I'm not one of them.

Terrell Davis
tailback (1992–94),
in September 1993

Garrison Hearst's understudy might be the second-best running back in the SEC. If not, he's certainly the SEC's best-kept secret.

Scott M. Reid
Atlanta sportswriter,
on Terrell Davis

He deserves a lot of credit for what we did. Terrell Davis does a lot of things the fans don't see.

Eric Zeier
quarterback (1991–94; captain 1993–94)

Terrell Davis is an inspiration to me because, though he was hurt at Georgia, he went on to the NFL and is very successful. He's someone I really look up to because he was in a situation similar to mine. But he turned it around and proved a lot of people wrong.

Robert Edwards
tailback (1993–94, 1996–97, captain 1996)

H e's been a really good back ever since he hit the scene. He's up there with Fred Taylor (Florida) and (Tennessee's) Jamal Lewis.

Terry Bowden
former Auburn coach/TV analyst,
on Robert Edwards

E verybody likes to have a guy who, when he gets the ball, everybody in the stadium stands up to see what's going to happen. Every time he touches the ball it kind of takes your breath away, because you know he can go all the way.

Jim Donnan
head coach (1996–2000),
on Robert Edwards

G eorgia is known as Tailback University, so people are more aware of who you are and what you do when you play tailback. It's just the position; if it was anybody, it'd be the same way.

Robert Edwards
1997 Tom Greene Award winner
(Middle Georgia football player of the year)

W e see it everyday in practice, but to see it in a game-type situation is pretty amazing. Sometimes, you find yourself just looking at him instead of blocking.

Matt Stinchcomb
tackle (1995–98),
on Robert Edwards

MAJOR
MOMENTS

T he Bulldogs shaded Tulane, 7–6, in a game which featured the longest punt in Georgia history. Bill Hartman booted it 82 yards from the line of scrimmage in a big play which kept the Greenies away from what could have been the winning touchdown.

Tom Little

author,
on Hartman's record-breaker,
recorded on November 13, 1937

BETWEEN THE HEDGES

It would smack of the absurd to try and place all the great moments in Georgia football history into a single chapter. A full-length book would be challenged to do so. The following pages attempt to touch on only some of the standout events that have graced the pages of Bulldog lore for well over 100 years.

From Catfish Smith and the '29 Dogs to Flatfoot Frankie and the '42 Orange Bowl triumph to Trippi's magnificence in the '43 Rose Bowl and '46 Oil Bowl to Tarkenton's magic against Auburn in '59 to the miracle of Belue to Scott in 1980 to the phenomenal "Comeback at the Outback" in 2000 to the SEC championship year of 2002 to Outback Bowl victors again in 2005 . . . herein lies a collection of Saturday heroics to thrill any Bulldogs follower.

L ittle Albie was never stopped but twice—once in 1929 by a Georgia football team and Sunday by death.

**Newspaper obituary
on Albie Booth**

legendary Yale quarterback

J OYOUS HYSTERIA HOLDS ATHENS IN HAPPY THRALLDOM.

***Atlanta Constitution* headline**

October 30, 1929, after Georgia's
15–0 upset of Yale

S mith did everything except sing the National Anthem.

Tom Little

on Catfish Smith's one-man virtuosity in the
Bulldogs' stunning upset of Yale, at the Sanford
Stadium dedicatory game, October 29, 1929

Y ale didn't play anybody anywhere but in their bowl. You went to them; they didn't come to you. To have the Yale team come to Athens, Ga., and play a game of football was something that was absolutely unbelievable.

Herb Maffett

end (1928–30)

Catfish Eats Up
Little Albie, Yale
in 1929 Shocker

With the unveiling of Sanford Stadium, on October 29, 1929, came a dream game, an instant grid classic: Eastern powerhouse Yale vs. its southern nickname namesake, Georgia.

Led by diminutive star quarterback Albie Booth, the Bulldogs (Yale) never got untracked against an inspired Bulldog (Georgia) team, led by sensational sophomore end Vernon "Catfish" Smith. The final score: Smith 15, Yale 0.

Smith, whose fishy moniker emanated from a bet in high school when he devoured a whole catfish raw, blocked a Booth punt in the second quarter for a touchdown, before nailing Little Albie for a safety in the third period.

Capping off his singular performance, Catfish corralled halfback Spurgeon "Spud" Chandler's final-quarter 25-yard pass for yet another score.

His successful conversion after the first touchdown completed his 15-point total.

You get down there. The ball will be waiting for you.

Frank Sinkwich
*to wingback Lamar "Racehorse" Davis,
in the huddle preceding the final play
of the 1941 Auburn–Georgia game*

I still had the ball in my hand when the final gun went off and Lamar Davis broke right down the middle, and I threw it as far as I could, and he caught it, and we won 7–0. He caught it on the dead run and almost fell down, but he straightened up and went on.

Frank Sinkwich
*halfback (1940–42, captain 1942),
on the incredible ending to the '41
Auburn–Georgia game*

SINKWICH, RACEHORSE
BEAT THE CLOCK VS. AUBURN

For 59 minutes, the scoreboard in Columbus showed nothing but a pair of goose eggs for the 1941 clash of old rivals Georgia and Auburn.

With only seconds left, Auburn punted on what it believed would be the final play of the game, kicking away from dangerous Bulldog junior Frankie Sinkwich. Instead, the ball went out of bounds on the Georgia 35, leaving time for still one more play.

Fading back after the snap and drifting to his right, Sinkwich unleashed a cross-country aerial. Lamar "Racehorse" Davis, in a foot race with his defender, took the ball over his shoulder and went in for the improbable score.

The final whistle was never heard as shocked Georgia partisans thundered their approval at the 7–0 victory.

There being a singular lack of lions along the golden littoral of Florida, they fed the Texas Christians to the Georgia Bulldogs here this hot, steaming afternoon.

Ralph McGill
Atlanta Constitution, January 2, 1942,
on Georgia's 40–26 Orange Bowl win
over Texas Christian

That young fellow Sinkwich had quite a day, didn't he? From what I heard, he must have been playing the game almost by himself.

Judge Kenesaw Mountain Landis
major-league baseball commissioner,
after listening to the broadcast of the
1942 Orange Bowl game

E arly in the second quarter, Sinkwich made one of the most amazing plays of his career. Trying to run, he was completely surrounded by Texas defenders. Miraculously, he shot a pass to Ken Keuper, who pounded over the goal line. It was truly a remarkable play. It didn't seem possible Sinkwich could get the ball away. He seemed nailed for a certain loss. Instead, he threw a touchdown pass.

Jack Troy
Atlanta Constitution, January 2, 1942,
on Frank Sinkwich's brilliant Orange Bowl
performance the previous day

For one afternoon, the 34–0 victory over Georgia Tech in 1942 is the best game I ever saw. Tech was undefeated. We had lost only to Auburn. The winner was going to the Rose Bowl, and the SEC title was at stake. We did not make many mistakes that day.

Wally Butts

I saw Frankie Sinkwich late Friday night. He could barely walk, so bad were his ankles. How he ever played as much as he did is a mystery, except that he vowed he'd be in there as long as he could stand up.

Braven Dyer
Los Angeles Times, *January 3, 1943,*
after Sinkwich's gritty performance
in the Rose Bowl

I guess I have never had a better day in all my life.

Charley Trippi
*after his 1943 Rose Bowl MVP performance
vs. UCLA*

Van Davis—and boy, he's about the best ol' end playing anywhere—helped me suck out that UCLA end, and I didn't have anybody in my way. I got through in time to throw my hands in front of the ball, and it bounced back of the end zone.

Red Boyd
*tackle (1942),
whose block of a fourth-quarter Bob Waterfield
punt for a safety broke open the
1943 Rose Bowl game for Georgia*

I t was in the 1946 Oil Bowl that Trippi made the greatest punt return I ever saw. He started running to his right, reversed his field deep, ran over two Tulsa men at the 15, lowered the boom on another, and scored. He got just 68 yards, but he ran 108.

Wally Butts

S aturday's heroes are ofttimes even more impressive in Sunday's movies. . . . Lives there a football fan who doesn't know that Bill Herron is the boy who reached into the upset heavens and pulled down Francis Tarkenton's 13-yard pass in the last 30 seconds to beat Auburn Saturday afternoon?

Al Thomy
Atlanta Constitution, *November 16, 1959*

I t was a huge game—for the championship, the honor of Georgia, Coach Butts, and all of the good, great Baptists. The whole South was tuned in. I called a timeout but did not go to the sidelines to visit Coach Butts. We just didn't have any plays programmed for fourth-and-13 with 30 seconds to go and the whole reborn Confederacy hanging on the outcome. I drew up a play in the huddle. I actually did, just like the John R. Tunis books I grew up with.

Francis Tarkenton

on the improbable heroics that catapulted Georgia over Auburn, 14–13, in the closing seconds of their 1959 duel for the SEC championship

I 'll never forget the day Charlie Britt had in Jacksonville. He did it all. He passed to set up a surprising pass from Bobby Walden to Gorden Kelley. He anticipated a quick kick, dropped back on the snap, and returned it to the Florida 37. He then passed to Bobby Towns for a touchdown. He caught Bobby Joe Green from behind, then capped his great day by intercepting a pass and running it back 100 yards for a score. Thanks to Britt we won, 21–10.

Francis Tarkenton
on Britt's one-man performance
vs. Florida, November 7, 1959

Since the pass was low, it turned out to be an advantage. Alabama played a lot of pursuit and really came after me. When I got the ball off, I was immediately hit by several defenders, at least four or five, which took them out of the play. I didn't know what was happening until I heard the roar of the crowd. It was then that I knew Bob Taylor was going all the way.

Pat Hodgson

right end (1963–65),
on the infamous flea-flicker play from
quarterback Kirby Moore to end Hodgson
to tailback Bob Taylor, who sprinted 73 yards
for the touchdown that upset Alabama,
18–17, at Athens in 1965

We kicked Spurrier's ass. I still think I'm one of the reasons why he hates us so much. I was pounding his butt, whether he had the ball or not, all day long.

Bill Stanfill

*on the Bulldogs' 27–10 win over Florida
and Heisman Trophy-winner Steve Spurrier
in 1966*

Before 70,012 fans in the Gator Bowl arena, quarterback Mike Cavan gave a performance Florida Gators will not forget. In a phenomenal passing exhibition on a muddy field, Cavan directed Georgia to a 51–0 victory. When Cavan edged Ole Miss's Archie Manning as Sophomore of the Year, it was no surprise to Floridians. They were puzzled when Cavan was omitted from the consensus All-America Team.

Jesse Outlar

on Cavan's 1968 season

Florida in a standup–5. They may or may not blitz. They won't. Buck back, third down on the 8. In trouble . . . gonna pick up a block behind him . . . gonna throw on the run. Complete to the 25! Lindsay Scott, 35, 40! Lindsay Scott, 45, 50! Run, Lindsay! 25, 20, 15, 10, 5. . . . Lindsay Scott! Lindsay Scott! Lindsay Scott!

Larry Munson

Georgia radio play-by-play announcer,
on the legendary Belue-to-Scott miracle pass
that beat Florida, 26–21,
November 8, 1980

ou gotta make something out of nothing.

Buck Belue

quarterback (1978–81, captain 1981),
after his game-winning 93-yard scoring toss
to Lindsay Scott pulled out an improbable win
over Florida in 1980

I got to see Scott all the way. I was supposed to block the end, but when he dropped back, I just watched Scott and started running behind him. Yes, I was hollering.

Herschel Walker

who gained 238 yards on 37 carries in the 1980 Georgia–Florida game, all but forgotten in the aftermath of the legendary 93-yard scoring pass from Buck Belue to Lindsay Scott that produced a last-minute 26–21 Bulldogs win

With 1:03 showing on the scoreboard clock, Lindsay Scott wins the race. He crosses the goal line. It's gonna take a miracle. It *is* a miracle. They will shout it all day and the next and the next: "God is a Bulldog!"

Loran Smith
Lewis Grizzard

BELUE-TO-SCOTT
93-YARD TD TOSS
BURNS GATORS

Offensive coordinator George Haffner sent in a pass play designed to turn a possible first down for Georgia.

Only 1:20 remained in the 1980 "World's Largest Outdoor Cocktail Party"—Georgia vs. Florida at the Gator Bowl in Jacksonville—when Bulldogs quarterback Buck Belue looked over a third-and-11 situation from his own 7-yard line, with the Bulldogs down by a point, 21–20.

Spotting primary receiver Lindsay Scott at the 25, Belue waved the speedy receiver toward the open middle.

Scott pulled in the toss, turned, and sped down the left sideline past the stunned Gator defenders.

Ninety-three yards later, Scott had registered the game-winning touchdown and, along with Belue, a place in Bulldog history for the longest TD pass completion ever.

Realistically, you had to figure that Florida had won the game.

Vince Dooley

The pass that won the Florida game was a matter of doing what you were supposed to do. For years I had been drilled to catch the ball, tuck it, and get it upfield as quickly as possible. At the moment, I didn't expect it to go all the way, but it was something I had done for years in practice and games, so doing what I was supposed to do enabled me to score the biggest touchdown of my life.

Lindsay Scott
*wide receiver (1978–81,
offensive captain 1981)*

Georgia's luck in the 1981 Sugar Bowl bordered on the miraculous. They won by a touchdown, even though Notre Dame outgained them passing, 138 yards to 7, and rushing, 190 yards to 127. The remarkable thing about Georgia's rushing statistic was that freshman sensation Herschel Walker ran for 150 yards, while his mates totaled 23 yards in lost yardage.

Richard Whittingham

If there had been two Sugar Bowl MVP awards, and had it been up to me, I would have also given one to Scott Woerner.

Vince Dooley

FAST FACT: Woerner's interception in the 1980 national championship game against Notre Dame, with 2:56 remaining in the Sugar Bowl, sealed the Bulldogs' 17–10 victory. Herschel Walker garnered the game's official MVP award, with 150 rushing yards and two touchdowns.

P eople naturally want to know about the kick against Clemson. That distance is never a good percentage kick. You're 60 yards back, but it's something I was very confident about. I felt I was representing our whole team, and it was very important to make it. We had fought back, and it gave me more inspiration to make the kick. When I kicked it, I knew it was going to be long enough, but when there's 60 yards ahead of you, you just wait and see if the ball starts tailing off. I remember looking at holder Jimmy Harrell and seeing the smile on his face.

Kevin Butler

on his game-winning (and school record)
60-yard field goal that gave the Bulldogs
a 26–23 victory over Clemson in 1984

Kevin Butler

G lory, glory to ole Georgia!

John Lastinger
quarterback (1981–83),
after scoring the winning touchdown in
Georgia's 10–9 upset of top-ranked Texas
in the Cotton Bowl concluding the 1983 season

H e busted the ball. I'll bet the ball is flat.
He kicked the fool out of it.

Danny Ford
former Clemson head coach,
on Kevin Butler's SEC-record-tying 60-yard
field goal against the Tigers in 1984

In 60 minutes last Saturday, Robert Edwards accomplished what Herschel Walker, Garrison Hearst, and every other player in the history of Georgia football could not. In his first game as a running back, Edwards, a converted cornerback, scored a school-record five touchdowns as the Bulldogs won their season opener against South Carolina, 42–23.

Jack Carey
USA TODAY, September 8, 1995

He goes out and breaks a record that's stood for 102 or 103 years. I was shocked.

Ray Goff
quarterback (1974–76, captain 1976),
head coach (1989–95),
on Robert Edwards's five-touchdown debut
at running back in 1995

The fake punt is one of those deals that either works or it doesn't. We went from the outhouse to the penthouse.

Jim Donnan

October 16, 1999,
on a fake punt by Vanderbilt that backfired
early in the fourth quarter, on fourth-and-16
from the Vanderbilt 21, with VU leading, 17–10.
The play reversed Georgia's fortunes, and the
Bulldogs went on to win, 27–17

I'm going to say, "He threw it 100 yards and I had to fight off 30 men to catch it." It's the greatest football play I ever made in my life.

Randy McMichael
tight end (1999–2001)

FAST FACT: *Never in the history of college football's illustrious bowl games had a team come back from a 25-point deficit to win. Not until New Year's Day 2000, when the Dawgs, down to Purdue 25–0 less than five minutes into the second quarter of the Outback Bowl in Tampa, Florida, shut down the Boilermakers the rest of the way while miraculously registering 28 points, including kicker Hap Hines's 21-yard field goal in overtime, to defeat the Big Ten foe 28–25. The play of the game was delivered by tight end McMichael—a one-handed grab, with 1:19 remaining, of quarterback Quincy Carter's forced, off-balance pass into double-coverage for the tying score, after the ball had been deflected twice by Boilermaker defenders.*

David Greene ran his streak of consecutive passes without an interception to 206. That broke the SEC mark of 200 set in 1997 by Stewart Patridge of Mississippi. Greene's touchdown pass, a 1-yarder to Leonard Pope, was the 68th of his career, breaking the school record he had shared with Eric Zeier.

Associated Press

on two records that fell to David Greene during the Bulldogs' overwhelming 62–17 demolition of Kentucky, November 6, 2004, at Commonwealth Stadium. During that same game, Greene surpassed an NCAA Division I record, previously held by former Tennessee QB Peyton Manning, with his 40th career win. Greene ended his career with 42 victories as a starter

eorgia ball! Houdini's in the house!

Mark Jones

ESPN play-by-play announcer,
on 2005 Outback Bowl MVP David Pollack's
sack–strip–recovery of Wisconsin quarterback
John Stocco's fumble on the Georgia 5-yard line
with 5:38 left in the fourth quarter, preserving
the Dawgs' 24–21 victory

GEORGIA BULLDOGS ALL-TIME TEAM

*J*ohn Rauch, David Greene, "General" George Patton, Catfish Smith, Rex Robinson, Lars Tate, Garrison Hearst, Rodney Hampton, Terrell Davis—and those are just some of the players who didn't make it! The irony of every all-time team is that those not making the lineup are often more conspicuous than those legends selected.

Inevitably, the agony/joy of picking such a unit becomes an exercise in creativity. Despite the daunting presence of two Heisman Trophy winners at running back, it would be blasphemous to leave Charley Trippi off such an aggregation, so look deeper into his impressive resume. Trippi, considered the finest all-around athlete ever to enroll at Georgia, was unparalleled at defensive back, a position he brilliantly manned while carving out All-America credentials as a triple-threat tailback during the early to mid–1940s.

Some of these players are literally guys you'd go to war with, some having served in the Second World War. Through the ages, Georgia fans have been served a smorgasbord of superb athletic talent. Stand back, for this glittering array of the Red and Black's brightest will dazzle any Dawg.

THE ALL-TIME
GEORGIA BULLDOGS TEAM

OFFENSE

Terrence Edwards, *wide receiver*
George Poschner, *tight end*
Matt Stinchcomb, *tackle*
Pat Dye, *guard*
Ray Donaldson, *center*
Randy Johnson, *guard*
Edgar Chandler, *tackle*
Hines Ward, *wide receiver*
Francis Tarkenton, *quarterback*
Frank Sinkwich, *running back*
Herschel Walker, *running back*

DEFENSE

David Pollack, *defensive end*
Bill Stanfill, *defensive tackle*
Jimmy Payne, *defensive tackle*
Freddie Gilbert, *defensive end*
Richard Tardits, *linebacker*
Ben Zambiasi, *linebacker*
Boss Bailey, *linebacker*
Champ Bailey, *defensive back*
Charley Trippi, *defensive back*
Terry Hoage, *defensive back*
Jake Scott, *defensive back*
Bobby Walden, *punter*
Kevin Butler, *kicker*
Scott Woerner, *punt returner*
Gene Washington, *kick returner*
Vince Dooley, *coach*

TERRENCE EDWARDS
Wide Receiver (1999–2002)
All-SEC (2002)

Edwards already holds the school record for career receptions, receiving yards, and touchdown receptions, and he is rapidly nearing the top of the SEC record books in those same categories. Yet . . . I've heard Georgia head coach Mark Richt extol Edwards for his work ethic more than any other player—not a common trait in your average superstar.

Anne Milligan
writer,
The Red & Black

Edwards is a career leading receiver there and has been in some categories as a preseason All-American. He burned us three years ago down there with great explosiveness.

Lou Holtz
former head coach, South Carolina,
in 2002

GEORGE POSCHNER
Tight End (1940–42)
All-America (1942), All-SEC (1942)

Frankie Sinkwich refused to come to Georgia unless his bosom pal, George Poschner, also were given a scholarship. . . . In the opinion of people who knew football best, it was George Poschner and his uncanny talent at catching forward passes, running interference, and taking out would-be tacklers that made Sinkwich the most glamorous football star of his day.

Bill Stern

MATT STINCHCOMB
Tackle (1995, 1997–98)

All-America (1997, '98), All-SEC (1997, '98)

Stinchcomb epitomizes the student-athlete more than anyone in the country. You're talking about a lineman who has played guard and center, and one that was both an All-American by the coaches and an Academic All-American.

Jim Donnan

PAT DYE
Guard (1958–60, captain 1960)
All-America (1959, '60), All-SEC (1960)

The former highly successful head coach of Auburn, Dye was an alternate captain of the 1959 SEC champion Bulldogs, an ALL-SEC guard, and a two-time All-America selection. He figured in one of the most famous plays in Georgia history, in 1959 tipping a Florida pass ultimately intercepted and returned 100 yards for a touchdown by safety Charlie Britt, further moving Georgia down the road to its SEC championship.

RAY DONALDSON
Center (1977–79)

All-SEC (1979)

Donaldson, an excellent run-blocker, was first team All-SEC his senior year of 1979 in Athens, but that's nothing to what he accomplished over 17 seasons in the NFL, 13 of them with the Colts. Donaldson, a four-time consecutive Pro Bowler, in his 16th pro season anchored the offensive line of the 1995 Super Bowl champion Dallas Cowboys.

RANDY JOHNSON

Guard (1973–75, offensive captain 1975)

All-America (1975),
Birmingham Touchdown Club Award
(SEC Most Valuable Lineman, 1975),
All-SEC (1974, '75), Jacobs Award
(outstanding blocker in SEC, 1975)

Johnson was elected offensive captain in 1975 after helping the Bulldogs to a 9–2 regular season record and a Cotton Bowl berth. He was first team All-SEC in 1974 and '75, and was drafted by the NFL's Seattle Seahawks in 1976, where he played a season before going to Tampa Bay (1977, '78).

georgiadogs.com

EDGAR CHANDLER
Tackle (1965–67)
All-America (1966, '67), All-SEC (1966, '67),
Georgia Sports Hall of Fame (1988)

A two-time first-team All-American, Chandler played a key role in Georgia's three-year record of 23–9–0 from 1965 to 1967, including the 10–1 SEC and Cotton Bowl championship season of '66. Chandler went on to a six-year NFL career, five with the Buffalo Bills, where he was converted to linebacker to utilize his great speed. He was inducted into the State of Georgia Sports Hall of Fame in 1988 and died in 1992 after a long illness, at 46.

georgiadogs.com

HINES WARD

Wide Receiver (1994–97)

All-SEC (1997)

The versatile Ward, who wants to play wide receiver in the pros, enhanced his chances with 12 catches for 154 yards, both Outback Bowl records. "I'm still a rookie at it," said Ward, once a running back and quarterback, on receiving. "I'm having fun with it, a blast with it."

Jack Wilkinson

Atlanta Journal-Constitution,
*after the Bulldogs' overwhelming 33–6
Outback Bowl victory over Wisconsin
concluding the 1997 season, in which Ward's
future NFL receiving talents were on display*

FRANCIS TARKENTON

Quarterback (1958–60, captain 1960)

All-America (1960), All-SEC (1959, '60),
Pro Football Hall of Fame (1986)
College Football Hall of Fame (1987),
Atlanta Touchdown Club Award
(Southeast Area Back of the Year, 1959),
University of Georgia Athletic Association
Circle of Honor (1998)

Tarkenton has no superior as a field general and ball handler.

Wally Butts

He was the greatest quarterback ever to play the game.

Bud Grant

*head coach, Minnesota Vikings (1967–83),
on Fran Tarkenton*

FRANK SINKWICH

Halfback/Fullback (1940–42)

Heisman Trophy (1942), Walter Camp Award (1942),
All-America (1941, '42), All-SEC (1941, '42),
University of Georgia Athletic Association
Circle of Honor, jersey No. 21 retired (1943)

The greatest offensive back in modern intercollegiate football—and your record book will prove it—was Frank Sinkwich of the University of Georgia.

Undated magazine article, 1950s

Anytime a running back is mentioned in the same breath as Jim Thorpe, Red Grange, and Tom Harmon, everyone sits up and takes notice, and Sinkwich evoked such comparisons.

Furman Bisher

HERSCHEL WALKER

Tailback (1980–82)

Heisman Trophy (1982), Maxwell Award (1982),
Walter Camp Football Foundation National Player
of the Year (1982), All-America (1980, '81, '82),
All-SEC (1980, '81, '82), UPI National Back
of the Year (1980, '82), Nashville Banner Award
(SEC MVP, 1980, '81, '82), College Football
Hall of Fame (1999), jersey No. 34 retired (1985)

There has never been a story such as Herschel Walker in 1980. Frank Sinkwich didn't break in like this freshman from Wrightsville. Charley Trippi didn't either. O. J. Simpson had two years of junior college when he burst onto the scene, and Herschel surpassed Tony Dorsett's freshman performance with his 1,616 yards in 1980. The only one who was a blockbusting hero from beginning to end was Ozark Ike, and he played in the funny papers.

Loran Smith
Lewis Grizzard

I never get tired of running. The ball ain't that heavy.

Herschel Walker

DAVID POLLACK

Defensive End (2001–04)

All-America (2002, '03, '04), Ted Hendricks Award
(nation's top defensive end, 2003, '04),
Lombardi Award (nation's top lineman, 2004),
Bednarik Award (nation's top defensive player, 2004),
All-SEC (2002, '03, '04)

He's a great athlete. When you see him coming, you can't juke around. You've got to try and get away and get rid of the ball.

Andre Woodson
*Kentucky quarterback,
on Pollack*

David Pollack was, as usual, fantastic. That last play, where he ripped the ball out of the quarterback's hands and got it before it hit the ground, might have been the difference in the ballgame.

Mark Richt
*on Pollack's play of the game, preserving
Georgia's 24–21 win over Wisconsin
in the 2005 Outback Bowl*

Pollack plays only one way: like his hair is on fire.

Georgia assistant coach

BILL STANFILL

Defensive Tackle (1966–68)

All-America (1968), Outland Trophy
(nation's top interior lineman, 1968)
All-SEC (1967, '68)

At the time when he was playing, when he won the Outland Trophy, he was the only player who could absolutely stop the triple option, which at the time was unstoppable. Bill Yeoman of Houston once said he (Stanfill) was the only one who could take the dive player, the quarterback, and the pitch man all at once. With those long arms, I don't know that we ever had another player with the reach of Bill Stanfill.

Vince Dooley

JIMMY PAYNE
Defensive Tackle (1978–82)
All-America (1982), All-SEC (1980, '81, '82)

Payne, the only Bulldog in the modern era to letter in five seasons after being granted a medical redshirt in 1979, completed his career as Georgia's all-time sack leader, with 28 (since surpassed by Richard Tardits's 29). He and Freddie Gilbert formed the "Dynamic Duo" of Georgia's great early-1980s defenses. Payne, a three-time All-SEC first team selection, died of cancer in 1998, at 38.

georgiadogs.com

FREDDIE GILBERT
Defensive End (1980–83, captain 1983)

All-America (1983), All SEC (1982, '83)

A two-time All-SEC performer and four-year starter, Gilbert was part of the greatest four-year period in Georgia history, during which an overall record of 43–4–1 from 1980 to 1983 was posted. Gilbert's uncanny ability to put pressure on opposing quarterbacks netted him 26 career sacks, still fourth all time in Georgia's record book.

georgiadogs.com

RICHARD TARDITS
Linebacker (1985–88)
All-SEC (1988)

The most remarkable athlete ever to walk on at Georgia was Richard Tardits, the Frenchman who was one of the Silver Seniors of 1988. Richard's story, to me, is the most incredible in NCAA history.

Vince Dooley

FAST FACT: *Tardits, from Biarritz, France, had never played a down of American football before enrolling at UGA in 1985. His talent, competitive drive, and commitment ultimately earned him All-SEC honors his senior season. Tardits then went on to the NFL, playing the 1989 season with the Phoenix Cardinals and 1990–92 with the New England Patriots.*

BEN ZAMBIASI
Linebacker (1974–77)
All-America (1976), All-SEC (1976, '77)

Zambiasi nervously started to peak on Friday afternoons, and by Saturday he was so emotionally fired up that he would throw up before the kickoff without fail. The team ultimately became superstitious, not wanting to take the field until Ben had thrown up, and on one of those occasions they were nearly late for the kickoff, waiting for Ben to do his thing.

Loran Smith

He was another one of those relentless players. Just a wild, crazy man football player.

Vince Dooley
on Zambiasi

BOSS BAILEY
Linebacker (1998–99, 2001–02, captain 2002)
All-America (2002)

Brother of former UGA star Champ, Boss led the Dawgs in tackles in 2002 with 114, while recording six QB sacks and 9.5 tackles-for-loss. Voted the team's overall team captain, he was selected as a semi-finalist for both the Butkus (nation's outstanding linebacker) and Lombardi (nation's top lineman) awards. The 2002 Georgia defense finished first in the SEC and fourth nationally in scoring defense (15.4 ppg).

georgiadogs.com

CHAMP BAILEY
Cornerback (1996–98)
All-America (1998), All-SEC (1997, '98)

C hamp Bailey is the best all-around player in college football today. He'd be a top candidate for any of the national awards—best receiver, best defensive back, and the big one.

Mike Gottfried
*former Pitt head coach/TV analyst,
in 1997*

T his guy does things Charles Woodson never dreamed about.

Tony Barnhart
*ESPN/Atlanta Journal,
on Champ Bailey*

FAST FACT: *Woodson, a cornerback, was the 1997 Heisman Trophy winner.*

CHARLEY TRIPPI

Defensive Halfback (1942, '45, '46; captain 1946)

Maxwell Award (1946), All-America (1946),
Nashville Banner Award (SEC MVP, 1946),
Heisman Trophy runner-up (1946),
Atlanta Touchdown Club Award
(Southeast Area Back of the Year, 1946),
University of Georgia Athletic Association
Circle of Honor, jersey No. 62 retired (1947)

Trippi was the best defensive back I have seen in college or pro ball. I am a rather attentive observer on the football field, and I never saw Charley miss a tackle. They did not run by him.

Wally Butts

Trippi hit me on the goal line in the Oil Bowl, and it was the hardest lick I remember in football. I didn't remember it then. I was looking at the sky and wondering what had struck me.

Camp Wilson
Tulsa fullback

TERRY HOAGE

Defensive Back (1980–83)

All-America (1982, '83), All-SEC (1982, '83),
Atlanta Touchdown Club Award (Southeast Area
Back of the Year, 1983; co-winner 1982)

The best defensive player I've ever coached and maybe the best I've ever seen.

Vince Dooley

The guy's a ghost.

George MacIntyre
*former Vanderbilt University head coach,
on Hoage*

JAKE SCOTT

Defensive Back (1967–68)

Consensus All-America (1968), All-SEC (1967, '68),
State of Georgia Sports Hall of Fame (1986),
Nashville Banner Award (SEC MVP, 1968)

J ake Scott even loved practice. He was a student of the game, an athlete blessed with marvelous physical flexibility, speed, and quickness and was likely to make the big play at any time. When he was SEC Player of the Year in 1968, we made up a highlight reel of his big plays for the season. He made at least one big play—one that influenced the outcome of the game defensively—in every game. Jake, a maverick off the field, was one of the greatest players we had here at Georgia.

Vince Dooley

J ake Scott was an instinctive player. He had a knack for the ball. He understood tendencies like no one else.

Bob Griese

*Pro Football Hall of Fame quarterback,
Miami Dolphins*

BOBBY WALDEN
Punter (1958–60)

Walden still ranks as the No. 2 punter in Bulldog history, having carved out a 42.8-yard career average. His productivity is noteworthy for the fact that he also doubled as starting right halfback during Georgia's SEC championship season in 1959. Walden, who went on to punt for 14 seasons in the NFL, still holds the Georgia single-game mark for highest punting average, when he unloaded three kicks against Texas in 1958 for 189 yards—a phenomenal 63.0 average.

KEVIN BUTLER

Kicker (1981–84)

All-America (1983, '84), All-SEC (1981, '83, '84)
Birmingham Quarterback Club Award
(Most Valuable SEC Senior, 1984),
SEC Rookie of the Year (*Jacksonville Journal*, 1981)

No doubt, the greatest kicker of all. He had total confidence all the time. During every ball game, whenever we got past the 40-yard line, you could see Kevin walking in front of me, rolling his eyes. I knew what was on his mind. He knew that I knew.

Vince Dooley
on Butler

SCOTT WOERNER

Punt Returner (1977–80

All-America (1980), All-SEC (1979, '80),
Atlanta Touchdown Club Award
(1980 Southeast Area Back of the Year)

I think he could actually hear the foot-
steps bearing down on him when he was
fielding a punt, but that is why he was so
great. He never took his eyes off the ball.
He could concentrate so well, he could feel
what was going on around him. He wanted
to return punts.

Bill Lewis

*on 1980 All-America defensive back/
punt returner Woerner*

GENE WASHINGTON
Kick Returner (1973–76)

While the former flankerback is best known for partic-ipating in the infamous shoestring plays and end-arounds that resulted in spectacular touchdowns for Georgia in the mid–1970s, Washington still ranks at the top of the heap all time among UGA kick returners. For more than a quarter of a century, his marks, which include most kickoff returns, most return yards, and most touchdowns on kick returns, have ruled the record books in Athens. His 1,637 career kickoff return yards total exceeds the runner-up in that category by almost 500 yards.

VINCE DOOLEY

Head Coach (1964–88)

National championships (1968, 1980),
SEC championships (1966, '68, '76, '80, '81, '82),
NCAA Coach of the Year (1980), College Football
Hall of Fame (1994), Georgia Sports
Hall of Fame (1978)

There's no Lombardi hellfire and brimstone in him. He never raises his voice or challenges your courage or manhood. He never tries to con you or give you a sad story so you will play on your emotions. What he does is treat you like a man. . . . He says, "Here's what's in front of you, here's the plan the coaches have, but you're the one that has to do it."

Chip Wisdom
on Vince Dooley

Coach Dooley had told us we could play with anybody, and we believed him.

Bob Taylor
tailback (1963–65)

THE GREAT GEORGIA TEAMS

I t would have been interesting to see Trippi competing against Doc Blanchard and Glenn Davis of Army, but neither Coach Red Blaik nor Coach Frank Leahy (Notre Dame) was interested in playing that Georgia team.

Wally Butts
on the 1946 Bulldogs

I n his first season as head coach, Herman J. Stegeman, a former University of Chicago player who Amos Alonzo Stagg called the best all-around player he had coached, carried the Bulldogs to their first Southern championship and their first undefeated season since Pop Warner's 1896 team. The team featured one of the greatest lines that ever played in Athens, led by All-Southern players Owen Reynolds, A. M. Day, and Arthur Pew.

George Scherer
on the 1920 Red and Black

THE 1927 DREAM
AND WONDER TEAM

One of the early bright lights for Georgia football was Kid Woodruff's Dream and Wonder team of 1927.

Woodruff, a scrawny but ruggedly competitive five-year quarterback for the Red and Black (1907–08, 1910–12), coached the D&W team to Georgia's first national championship, topping the Poling and Boand polls of 1927.

A pair of All-America ends, Tom Nash and Chick Shiver, led the undefeated Bulldogs to nine straight wins that year, including an upset of Yale at New Haven—UGA's first-ever win over the Eli.

Heading into the regular-season finale against Georgia Tech, at Grant Field in Atlanta, Georgia was holding a Rose Bowl invitation in its hands. But Pasadena was not to be, as the Yellow Jackets burst the bubble of the Bulldogs' dream (not to mention their wonder), blanking UGA, 12–0.

THE FLAMING SOPHOMORES

In the 1929 Sanford Stadium dedicatory victory over Yale, a group of talented first-year varsity players emerged with a colorful nickname describing their amazing deeds: the Flaming Sophomores.

Heading the group was All-American Catfish Smith, the wunderkind end who scored all 15 points in the legendary upset of Yale, and a halfback who was credited with tossing Smith a touchdown pass that same afternoon, Spurgeon Chandler, later to gain renown as "Spud" Chandler, ace pitcher for the world champion New York Yankees and the American League's Most Valuable Player in 1943.

In their three-year run, the Flaming Sophomores helped the Bulldogs to an over-all record of 21–8–1, the best three-year cumulative total in Georgia football history to that point.

SINKWICH AND THE
1941 BULLDOGS—
BROKEN JAW AND ALL

In Coach Wally Butts's third year of guiding Georgia's fortunes, tailback sensation Flatfoot Frankie Sinkwich played every game but the opener with a broken jaw.

Sinkwich's unique jaw mask enabled him to continue playing and generated almost as much talk as his sterling play on the field. The Bulldog junior set a Southeastern Conference total offense record, in addition to leading the nation in rushing.

Upon posting a 9–1–1 season record, Georgia accepted its first-ever Bowl invitation—opposite TCU in the Orange Bowl.

Sinkwich single-handedly devastated the Horned Frogs, logging one of the most spectacular performances in bowl history: 243 yards passing, three touchdowns passes, 139 yards rushing, and one rushing touchdown, for an aggregate of 382 yards total offense.

The Bulldogs rolled, 40–26.

I can truthfully say that this is the only Georgia football team that has had the courage of a champion. Something always happened to the others. This one had what was necessary to come through—the courage of a champion.

Bulldog fan
on the 1941 Georgia team

The Georgia eleven, coached by Wally Butts, won its first Southeastern Conference title in 1942. Nevertheless, good as the Bulldogs were, the national championship went to the Buckeyes of Ohio State.

Robert Leckie
author

FAST FACT: *The Bulldogs actually finished atop six national polls recognized by the NCAA in 1942.*

T he chap who wrote "Georgia on My Mind" must have been thinking about the great Dixie football team which defeated UCLA, 9–0, yesterday in the famed Rose Bowl. Seldom has a Rose Bowl team rolled up such a commanding margin in first downs and yardage and emerged with so few points on the scoreboard. The Bruins can thank their lucky stars they got off as fortunately as they did.

Braven Dyer
Los Angeles Times, *January 2, 1943,*
on the 1942 Red and Black

Trippi made All-America lists in 1946, and he made Georgia forget Fireball Frank Sinkwich, as he led a great eleven to the school's first unbeaten, untied year since 1896.

Lamont Buchanan
on the 1946 Bulldogs

The 1946 team had a perfect record, averaged more than 20 points a game. It was a great team, but at the end of the 1941 season I think the Orange Bowl team that routed TCU was the best I coached. The 1942 Rose Bowl, the 1948 and 1959 Orange Bowl teams were also outstanding.

Wally Butts

The major preseason prognostications of 1959 pegged the University of Georgia no higher than ninth in the 12-team Southeastern Conference football race. By the time of the November 14 home date with Auburn, the Bulldogs would clinch the SEC crown if they could whip the Tigers. [Down 13–7 late in the fourth quarter] Tarkenton took to the air. The Bulldogs got to the Auburn 13, fourth down, with 30 seconds to play. Tarkenton dropped back and the eligible Georgia receivers flared out. Bill Herron broke free into the left hand corner of the end zone and Tarkenton hit him. Durward Pennington kicked the conversion for a 14–13 Georgia victory and the conference title.

Harold Claassen
on the 1959 Bulldogs

This is a team I will never forget. They truly paid the price to win. I would say they exploited maximum ability more than any of my teams. We had finished tenth in 1958, and the experts had moved us up no higher than ninth in the preseason polls. They wanted to be champions.

Wally Butts

on the 1959 SEC champion Bulldogs

After we began to win at Georgia, it was nice to go back home (to Alabama) and talk about my championship team. Respect. That is so important, and that is what Vince Dooley brought to us in 1964.

"General" George Patton

defensive tackle (1964–66, captain 1966)

Bill Stanfill remembers fondly the defense coming off the field to chants of "DAMN GOOD TEAM! DAMN GOOD TEAM!"

Marc Weiszer

Morris News Service,
on the 1966 Bulldogs

We've had championship teams, certainly much better teams, but in all sincerity I've never been prouder of a football team at Georgia than I was of the 1973 squad. They had the pride to come back, and that's what this game is all about.

Vince Dooley

We began the 1978 season knowing that we could make the chapel bell ring on Saturdays, and we did.

Willie McClendon

on the 9–2–1 Bulldog team that he captained
in 1978, a team Coach Dooley said was
the worst group of seniors he had ever had

This is the fightingest football team I've ever coached.

Vince Dooley

on his 1980 national champion
Georgia Bulldogs

I told you before the game that you had more character and unity than any team I've been around, and I loved you. I'm gonna tell you again—you have more character and unity than any team I've ever been around, and I love you!

Vince Dooley

to his 1980 national championship team
in the locker room following the 1981
Sugar Bowl triumph over Notre Dame

After losing Herschel to the USFL, we would play the 1983 season without a running back. To get the mileage out of that 1983 team that we did was remarkable. This team upset No. 1 Texas in the Cotton Bowl for the 10–9 victory that ranks as one of the greatest upsets by a Georgia team.

Vince Dooley

T he Bulldogs cost fans throughout the state their fingernails several times this fall, but Georgia's 12–1 ride to the Southeastern Conference championship is one of the most memorable sports moments in 2002.

Gentry Estes
Albany (Ga.) Herald

H opefully the whole Bulldog nation will always remember this senior class because we did a great job. Three years in a row: 10-win seasons. You couldn't ask for anything better than that.

Fred Gibson
on the 2002–04 Bulldog teams

FIELDS
OF PLAY

H elp make our old red-dirt field . . . one of the best athletic fields in the South.

Dr. Charles Herty

HERTY FIELD

Dr. Herty's "old red-dirt field" originated in the fall of 1891.

The doctor helped students prepare the playing field and oversaw the leveling of its surface. The University Glee Club made a memorable contribution to the cause, donating $50 "to finance removal of rocks and the filling in of the worst holes."

Crude goalposts were erected at the ends of the field, which measured 110 yards.

In 1897, Herty raised $1,900 from Georgia alumni that went to grading, seeding the field, and building bleachers. The outcome was "one of the best athletic fields in the South," according to Herty.

The remodeled gridiron was christened Alumni Athletic Field but after several years became known as Herty Field.

S mall boys . . . began to climb up on the roofs of the houses around the grounds. Soon they lined every point of vantage that allowed the slightest view of the grounds. They looked like black birds squatted on top of the houses and perched up on the limbs of trees.

Atlanta Constitution

preceding the 1896 Auburn–Georgia clash at Brisbane Park in Atlanta, where more than 8,000 spectators, at the time the largest crowd south of Philadelphia to see a college football game, attended. Two legendary coaches squared off that day: Georgia's Pop Warner and Auburn's John Heisman, both in the early years of their storied careers. UGA gained its second victory in five years over Auburn, 12–6

PIEDMONT PARK, BRISBANE PARK, ATHLETIC PARK

Three fields in Atlanta served as home for the Red and Black's big games in the 1890s.

Piedmont Park, on the eastern border of the exposition grounds of the 1896 World's Fair, was originally graded for Buffalo Bill's Wild West Show. Before the Fair, the park had hosted the inaugural Auburn–Georgia clash, on February 20, 1892.

Brisbane Park, in south Atlanta, hosted Georgia's 1896 season-opening 26–0 victory over Wofford. The field was located on the block surrounded by Glenn, Ira, Crumley, and Windsor Streets.

Athletic Park, on Jackson Street, just off Auburn Avenue, was the site of the 1894 Auburn–Georgia game. Georgia's 10–8 win that day was its first victory ever over Auburn.

Much of the valley between the Franklin and Agricultural College campuses was only a wild bottomland, a picturesque but marshy dale. On either side of a little stream, called Tanyard Creek, were sharply rising banks covered by a forest of giant trees. . . . Professor Steadman Vincent Sanford wasn't interested so much in the beauty of the scene as with a vision that was haunting him: a natural bowl with a football field in the hollow. The reverie of this kindly English teacher and the administrative energy of the same man years later were largely responsible for the transformation of that damp and shadowy valley into the beautiful Sanford Stadium of today.

John F. Stegeman

eorgia now had a new playing field, which lay in the Tanyard Creek hollow just off Lumpkin Street, a few hundred yards west of the future stadium site. The new ground, a combination baseball diamond and football field, named for Director Sanford, boasted a covered grandstand. It was considered one of the most handsome fields in the South.

John F. Stegeman
on Sanford Field, 1911

FAST FACT: The grandstand seated 3,500.

e had a good groundskeeper and a good field. We had old wooden stands on one side. The fans would drive their automobiles up to 15 feet from the sidelines and sit in their cars and watch the game.

Buck Cheves
on Sanford Field

I have played in many stadiums, but to me there are only two special stadiums—Yankee Stadium in New York and Sanford Stadium in Athens, and there is no comparison between the two. There is no place in the world precisely like the grass that grows between the hedges in Athens, Georgia.

Francis Tarkenton

Sanford Stadium

The inspiration of UGA faculty chairman of athletics Dr. S. V. Sanford, Sanford Stadium was completed in time for a memorable debut, on October 12, 1929, against eastern powerhouse Yale.

It was fitting that the Eli be invited as Georgia's first opponent in the new facility. In addition to sharing the same nickname, Bulldogs, both schools employed the same architects—Atwood & Nash—to design their respective stadiums.

Originally a 30,000-seater, Sanford Stadium went through expansions to 38,400, then 54,000.

Today it houses the famed hedges that encircle what was once termed "the finest turfed gridiron in America," and seats 92,746 spectators, making it the fifth-largest on-campus college venue in the United States.

THE RIVALRIES

Rivalries start with a feeling, a strong feeling usually not commensurate with brotherly love. For followers of the early Red and Black, this feeling originated with the very first Auburn–Georgia game, played at Piedmont Park in Atlanta in the late winter chill of 1892.

Sometimes, as was the case that fateful day of February 20, a sorrowful loss fuels the fires of a budding rivalry. Partisan faces were long and spirits dampened after the Plainsmen laid a 10–0 loss on Georgia that afternoon.

Other intense rivalries would follow: Georgia Tech and Florida most prominently, while Clemson, South Carolina, Alabama, and Tennessee all have rankled the Bulldog nation through the years.

Step onto the field of heated feuding. Feel the tension, let the war begin.

I t's been said that football is the secular religion of the South. If so, then the gridiron grudge between the University of Georgia and the Georgia Institute of Technology is nothing less than the genesis myth, the creation of good and evil.

John Chandler Griffin

author

One end of the field had been plowed and there were plenty of earth clods on the ground. Some small boys did throw them. One of these evidently had a rock in it and when it struck Wood just over his right eye it made a gash about three inches long. That didn't bother Wood. He would just wipe his bleeding brow and then plaster the face of some Georgia player with a handful of blood. He seemed to take delight in grabbing two Georgia boys and bumping their heads together. He just ran roughshod over everybody in front of him.

T. W. Reed

spectator,
at the first Georgia–Georgia Tech game,
in 1893 at Herty Field in Athens

FAST FACT: *Tech had augmented its roster with several northern "ringers," one of whom, 33-year-old U. S. Army surgeon Captain Leonard Wood, wreaked one-man havoc on the Red and Black all afternoon. Georgia Tech overwhelmed UGA, 28–6.*

F our years following the riot of 1893, school officials felt it was finally safe for Georgia and Georgia Tech to resume their series. On October 23, 1897, these two hated rivals went at it once again.

John Chandler Griffin

FAST FACT: The Bulldogs evened the series at 1–1, with a convincing 28–0 drubbing of Tech.

I saw hate in a lot of people's eyes. It's exactly the type rivalry I thought it was.

Buck Belue
on Georgia–Georgia Tech

LO, THE DREADED DROUGHT

From 1948 to 1957, "the Drought" cursed the land of the Bulldogs—the years when archrival Georgia Tech reeled off an eight-game consecutive win streak over Georgia.

Athenians waited interminably for a knight in Red and Black to carry high UGA's colors once more. Their gladiator eventually came, wearing No. 40 and calling himself a Sapp.

On November 30, 1957, in Atlanta, Bulldog fullback Theron Sapp single-handedly reversed the withering downward spiral with a radiant performance that overnight made him a Georgia legend and ultimately placed him in the highest echelon of Bulldog greats—alongside Frank Sinkwich, Charley Trippi, and Herschel Walker—as one of only four players in UGA history to have his jersey number retired.

After a scoreless first half, with the Yellow Jackets in possession of the ball midway through the third period, Sapp fell on a fumble by Tech's Floyd Faucette. The workhouse Sapp then carried the ball nine times for 35 yards on the ensuing 50-yard drive for Georgia, diving up the middle to score the game's lone touchdown that finally ended the long dry spell.

A tlanta will be the scene Saturday afternoon of the first Southern interstate intercollegiate football game. . . . Both teams have been in training for several weeks. Both are uniformed and well-equipped. Both have been studying the game from a scientific as well as a physical standpoint, and the contest promises to be a very close and interesting one.

Atlanta Journal
February 17, 1892,
on the inaugural Georgia–Auburn game

I t was the most thrilling game of football ever played in the Southern states—a game the likes of which for intense excitement and clever playing on both sides will hardly ever be seen again, perhaps never on the Southern field.

Remson Crawford
Atlanta Constitution, *February 1892,*
on the first Auburn–Georgia game

BEAT AUBURN OR QUIT THE GAME.

Sign in Georgia dressing room
hung by UGA players, 1901

It is the biggest victory Georgia has won in years.

Harry Hodgson
Atlanta Constitution,
*after Georgia's 0–0 tie with Auburn
in 1901*

They'll talk of how halfbacks Fred Brown and Captain Don Soberdash kept Bulldog drives percolating with dedicated slashes through the line, how Charlie Britt returned a punt 30 yards through Auburn's first team for a touchdown behind Dye's key block, how Bill Godfrey smashed for important short yardage, how Bobby Walden kept kicking the Tigers back until Britt made his third-quarter run, how Bobby Towns got open for passes and first-down runs . . . and how the cool, confident right arm of Francis Tarkenton capped it with a perfect pass in the last 30 seconds.

Al Thomy
Atlanta Constitution,
*on Georgia's miraculous last-minute, 14–13 win
over Auburn to take the 1959 SEC title*

It was one of the greatest games a Georgia team has played.

Wally Butts
on the 1959 Auburn game for the
SEC championship

Auburn had 11 All-Americans out there. We could not have beaten them with one or two All-Americans. We needed 11 to match them.

Pat Dye
after the legendary Auburn game of '59

Georgia just gave us a good old-fashioned licking, a physical beating. Larry Rakestraw is the best quarterback we've seen. I salute them for their good play.

Shug Jordan
Auburn head coach (1951–75),
following the 30–21 loss to Georgia in 1962

The Alabama–Georgia rivalry is one of the most colorful and longest in southern football annals. A Rose Bowl assignment was on the line when the two collided at Atlanta, October 31, 1942. Both clubs had spotless records. Offense-minded Georgia, with Frankie Sinkwich, had become the toast of Dixie. Georgia turned defeat into victory, 21–10, with a 21-point last quarter outburst which still ranks as one of the great moments on Dixie gridirons. Sinkwich completed 17 of 33 passes for 230 yards in a flurry which Alabama just couldn't handle.

Harold Claassen
author/former Associated Press editor

B uck Cheves was the whole show in Georgia's backfield. He is greased lightning and the fastest starting back in Southern football.

Birmingham News
*after Georgia's 21–14 defeat of Alabama,
November 20, 1920, one of the most revered
victories in Bulldog annals*

T he Georgia–Florida series developed a reputation for its smash-mouth brand of football on the field and two-fisted bourbon-laced partying in the stands.

Derek Smith

B y the late 1950s, *Florida Times-Union* sports editor Bill Kastelz described [the Georgia–Florida game] as the "world's largest outdoor cocktail party."

Derek Smith

The way I had it figured, I'd been preparing for this game for seven years. I started going hard in junior high school, then moved up to high school, then to college to get right here, undefeated, against Florida, a team we had never beaten. We couldn't have lost it today.

Royce Smith
guard (1969–71, captain 1971)

FAST FACT: Smith's Bulldogs resoundingly beat the John Reaves/Carlos Alvarez-led Florida Gators team of 1971, 49–7.

The revelry is bawdy, raucous, and always unpredictable; but without the tradition born between the sidelines there would be no party. The fans' antics will never overshadow feats such as Georgia back Charley Trippi's five-touchdown performance in 1942.

Derek Smith
on Georgia–Florida

We really don't hate each other; we're competitors. No matter who we're playing, we want to beat them. Whether it's little sisters in the pool, we want to beat them.

David Pollack
defensive end (2001–04),
on rivalries

YOU GOT THE HUNCHBACK!
WE GOT THE TAILBACK!

Cheer heard on Bourbon Street
in New Orleans on the eve of the
1981 Sugar Bowl for the national championship
between the Fighting Irish of Notre Dame and the
Herschel Walker-led Georgia Bulldogs

THE
LOCKER ROOM

One afternoon, with his overconfident team taking a licking and time running out, an exasperated Coach Wally Butts lost his temper and yelled down the bench to a substitute, "Hey, fathead, get into the game!" But not a man on the Georgia bench moved. Finally the timid voice of a sub piped up: "Which fathead, coach?"

Bill Stern

TOWNS'S OAK TREE

The oak tree that for 31 years took root behind the president's box at Sanford Stadium was a gift from a most unlikely donor.

Legendary UGA athlete, Forrest "Speck" Towns, a former world record-holder in the 110-meter high hurdles, was presented a seedling oak by the Fuhrer himself, Adolf Hitler, for his gold-medal performance in the high hurdles at the 1936 Olympic Games in Berlin.

Towns returned to play end for the Bulldogs in both the 1936 and '37 seasons.

In 1967, the oak was transferred to a location near Stegeman Coliseum to make room for Sanford Stadium's upper deck.

Though the original tree failed to survive the move, a first-generation seedling from the oak was replanted and still thrives today.

John Unitas was the first great contemporary quarterback Francis Tarkenton followed when he was crafting his own game in high school at Athens and at the University of Georgia. He observed him on television, and envied the strength of his arm and the late-game heroics that became the wellspring of the Unitas cult.

Jim Klobuchar
author

I can't stand Auburn, I despise Florida, and Georgia Tech ain't even worth wasting a breath on. But I hate Notre Dame.

Georgia man
New Year's Eve on Bourbon Street, the evening before the 1980 national championship game between Notre Dame and Georgia

S mith, there are two things that don't go in the Yale Bowl, and roughness is one of them.

Albie Booth
Yale quarterback (1929–31)

A nd you are the other.

Vernon "Catfish" Smith
end (1929–31)

FAST FACT: All-America UGA end Catfish Smith had dogged Booth, Yale's legendary QB, all afternoon on October 10, 1931. After repeated tackles for losses by the physical Smith, Booth blurted out the above, precipitating Smith's return wisecrack.

You're just a bunch of dollar football players.

Harry Mehre
*head coach (1928–37),
to his Bulldog squad in the locker room of the
Yale Bowl in 1931, during the Depression era,
when Yale ticket prices ranged in scale from
expensive (vs. Harvard) to cheap (for the
Georgia game). Georgia trounced Yale, 26–7*

The Columbia quarterback got to his feet and proceeded to line up with the Georgia team.

Bill Stern
*on Columbia University QB Thornley Wood,
who, in the 1941 game against Georgia, took a
hard blow to the head but informed the team
doctor that he was okay to remain in the game*

In 1950, the Associated Press conducted a poll of 391 sportswriters and broadcasters to determine the greatest college football player of the first half of the twentieth century. Charley Trippi finished eighth.

Richard Whittingham

Trippi is tops. The Bruins, linemen and backs alike, said Charley's terrific drive, high knee action, pivoting, and change of pace were the best they'd ever seen.

Associated Press

*following the 1943 Rose Bowl, the 9–0
Georgia shutout of UCLA for the 1942
national championship*

IRONMAN CHAMP

Versatile UGA 1998 consensus All-America cornerback Champ Bailey became the first three-way starter for Georgia in four decades, when the talented sophomore opened up on both offense and defense, in addition to special teams, on October 18, 1997, in a game against Vanderbilt in Nashville.

Bailey, the regular left corner, lined up at flanker opposite the Commodores, catching two passes for 59 yards. He also had one rush for four yards. But that wasn't all for the gifted junior. Bailey also returned the opening kickoff 33 yards, making it a unique hat trick, position-wise, for the evening.

Bailey's achievement was the first of its kind in 38 years for a Bulldog player, dating back to the 1959 season.

One of the best things I remember about playing at Georgia was the excitement of looking up into the stands and seeing 85,000 fans. Game day was really special and the encouragement from the fans was great. It was an unbelievable experience.

Garrison Hearst

running back (1990–92),
All-America (1992),
1992 Doak Walker Award winner

Quit looking up there! The game is out here!

Vince Dooley

to his Bulldogs in the 1981 Sugar Bowl at the Superdome. It seems the Georgia players were mesmerized watching replays of themselves on the massive indoor TV screens hanging over the field

A lot of things happen when you are sleeping. I don't want to miss anything. Something exciting might happen, and I would hate to sleep through it.

Herschel Walker
*who used to average only a few hours
of sleep per night*

S till doing the same thing. It really hasn't changed much. I think I'm fooling myself to think I'm still young. I'm gonna be the George Foreman of football and at 70, I'll come back.

Herschel Walker
*who, at age 40 in 2002, still tackled a daily
workout regimen of 1,500 pushups and
2,000–3,000 sit-ups*

This has been the best four years of my life. Don't cry because it's over. Smile.

David Pollack

following the 2005 Outback Bowl 24–21 win over Wisconsin, Pollack's final game for UGA

If I'd known when I was two what it was like down South, I would have crawled down here.

Frank Sinkwich

1942 Heisman Trophy winner from Youngstown, Ohio

YOU CAN"T SPELL 'SUGAR' WITHOUT 'UGA'!

Chant from 12,000 Bulldog fans

at the conclusion of Georgia's 31–21 win over Auburn in 1980 to clinch the SEC championship

GEORGIA
NATIONAL CHAMPION
ROSTERS

Bulldog followers may think that the 1980 national championship team under Vince Dooley is the only national crown in Georgia annals, but the 'Dogs have copped various national titles as far back as 1927. True, the '80 season was the only consensus crown, but these names from other glory years should not be forgotten. The champion Red and Black.

1927

9–1

National champions in Poling and Board polls
George Woodruff, *Head Coach*

Player	Pos.
Boland, Joe H.	C
Broadnax, John E.	QB
Dudley, Frank C.	HB
Estes, Roy E.	HB
Frisbie, Theodore	T
Haley, Eugene	G
Hooks, Bobby	HB
Jacobson, Roy H.	G
Johnson, H. F. Jr.	QB
Lanford, Leroy	C
Lautzenhiser, Glen	T
McCrary, Herdis W.	FB
McTigue, Robert E.	HB
Morris, J. Robert	T
Nash, Tom A.	E
Palmer, Henry G.	E
Rothstein, Bennie	FB
Shiver, Ivy M. Jr. "Chick"	E
Smith, Eugene	G
Stelling, Cree	T

1942

11–1

(includes 9–0 Rose Bowl win over UCLA)
National champions in DeVold, Houlgate, Litkenhous, Poling, and Berryman polls
Wally Butts, *Head Coach*

Player	Pos.	Wt.	Ht.	Yr.
Anderson, Alfred	E	190	6–2	Jr
Dudish, Andy	WB	171	5–11	Sr
Boyd, Willard	T	207	5–11	So
Costa, Leo	C/K	180	5–10	Sr
Davis, Lamar "Racehorse"	**E/WB**	**185**	**6–1**	**Sr**
Davis, Van	**E**	**195**	**6–0**	**Sr**
Ehrhardt, Clyde	**C**	**201**	**6–1**	**Jr**
Ellenson, Gene	**T**	**197**	**6–1**	**Sr**
Godwin, Bill	C	215	6–1	Jr
Grate, Carl	G	202	6–0	Jr
Harrison, Norman	BB	183	6–0	So
Heyn, Clarence	G	180	6–0	So
Keuper, Kenneth	BB	197	6–0	Sr
Kuniansky, Harry	**G**	**185**	**5–10**	**Sr**
Landry, Bob	BB	199	6–0	So
Lee, Jim	G	182	6–0	Jr
Lee, Ryals	TB	165	6–0	Jr

BB—Blocking Back   WB—Wingback   **Starters in bold**

Player	Pos.	Wt.	Ht.	Yr.
Maguire, Walter	BB	179	6–0	Jr
McClure, Ardie	T	197	6–2	So
McPhee, Dick	**FB**	**186**	**5–11**	**Jr**
Miller, J. P.	G	186	5–10	Jr
Nunnally, Jerry	WB	170	5–11	Jr
Peters, Vernon	T	202	5–11	So
Phelps, Morris	E	180	5–11	Sr
Pierce, Brooke	T	206	5–11	Jr
Plant, Frank	C	196	6–0	So
Polak, Joe	BB	181	5–9	Jr
Poschner, George	**E**	**183**	**6–0**	**Sr**
Poss, Bob	T	201	5–11	So
Pounds, Jack	WB	156	5–9	So
Richardson, Dick	T	190	6–0	So
Ruark, Walter	**G**	**191**	**5–11**	**Sr**
Sinkwich, Frank	**TB/FB**	**185**	**5–10**	**Sr**
Strother, Clinton	E	197	6–3	So
Tereshinski, Joe	E	190	6–2	So
Todd, Jim	FB	181	6–1	Sr
Trippi, Charley	**TB/FB**	**181**	**6–0**	**So**
Vickery, Farrar	E	185	6–0	So
Williams, Garland	**T**	**195**	**6–2**	**Jr**

1946

11–0

(includes 20–10 Sugar Bowl victory over North Carolina)
National champions in Williamson poll

Wally Butts, *Head Coach*

Player	Pos.
Alexander, Eugene	G
Bradberry, George	B
Bray, Mell	B
Bush, Jackson	**T**
Chandler, Eugene Jr.	C
Chesna, Joe	C
Cook, Johnny	B
Cooley, Michael	**C**
Deavers, Clayton	C
Deleski, Gerald	C
Donaldson, John	B
Edwards, Dan	**E**
Ford, George	B
Fordham	**E**
George, Carl	**G**
Geri, Joe	B
Griffith, John	B
Hague, Bobby	B
Henderson, William	B
Hobbs, Homer	G
Hodges, Billy	B

BULLDOG MADNESS

Player	Pos.
Jeffrey, Al	G
Jenkins, Donald	T
Jernigan, George T.	G
Johnson, Howard "Moose"	G
Kaminski	B
Lee, Ryals	B
Maricich, Eli	B
McCue	C
McPhee, Richard	**FB**
Moseley, Reid Jr.	E
Nestorak, Stan	B
Payne, Porter	G
Perhach, Andrew	T
Rauch, John	**QB**
Richardson, Dick	G
Sellers, Weyman	E
Singletary, Wilson Eugene	T
Smith, Charles H.	**RHB**
St. John, Herbert	**G**
Taylor, Spafford	B
Tereshinski, Joe	**E**
Terry, John	T
Tiller	E
Trippi, Charley	**LHB**
Williams, Garland	**T**

1968

8–1–2

(includes 16–2 Sugar Bowl loss to Arkansas)
National champions in Litkenhous poll
Vince Dooley, *Head Coach*

Player	Pos.	Wt.	Ht.	Yr.
Adkins, Ronnie	LG	225	6–3	So
Allen, Ed	WB	166	5–8	So
Baker, Sam	RT	233	6–4	So
Boggus, Stan	DB	175	5–11	Jr
Brannen, Millard	RT	225	5–11	Jr
Brasher, Larry	DT	215	6–2	So
Brice, Billy	**TE**	**210**	**6–4**	**So**
Brown, Steve	DL	208	5–11	So
Byrd, Wayne	**RT**	**225**	**6–1**	**Jr**
Callaway, Harold	FB	202	6–0	So
Callaway, Tim	**DL**	**210**	**6–1**	**Jr**
Campbell, Johnny	TB	185	5–9	So
Carnes, Max	S–PK	187	5–10	So
Cavan, Mike	**QB**	**190**	**6–1**	**So**
Chamberlain, Steve	C	216	6–1	So
Chandler, Bob	P	185	6–2	Jr
Clamon, Joe	DL	215	6–2	Jr
Couch, Tommy	LB	205	6–1	So
Daniel, Lee	**DT**	**195**	**6–2**	**Sr**
Darby, Bill	DB	182	5–10	So
Davis, Glenn	QB	195	6–0	So
Dicks, Happy	**LB**	**210**	**6–2**	**Sr**
Dumbleton, Ken	RT	220	6–3	So
DuPriest, Bob	LB–C	188	5–10	Jr
Elrod, Craig	WB	195	6–1	Jr
Epperson, Rusty	FB	195	5–11	Jr
Farnsworth, Steve	TB	210	6–1	Jr
Gilbert, Paul	QB	183	6–0	Jr
Gordon, Hugh	DL	215	5–11	So

BULLDOG MADNESS

Player	Pos.	Wt.	Ht.	Yr.
Graham, Don	QB	185	6–2	So
Greene, Mike	TE	210	6–3	So
Greer, Steve	**DL**	**215**	**6–0**	**Jr**
Griffin, John	DB	180	5–11	Jr
Hampton, Donnie	QB	183	6–0	Jr
Henderson, Terry	S	195	6–1	So
Herlong, Greg	DE	195	6–2	Jr
Huggins, Ronnie	**LB**	**195**	**5–8**	**Jr**
Hughes, Dennis	TE	220	6–1	Jr
Hurley, James	DE	200	6–0	So
Jennings, John	LG	210	6–0	So
Johnson, Brad	**FB**	**205**	**5–11**	**Sr**
Johnson, Fred	DT	225	6–3	Jr
Johnson, Sandy	DE	200	6–2	Sr
Jones, Spike	**P**	**180**	**6–2**	**Jr**
Kemp, Bruce	**WB**	**210**	**6–3**	**Jr**
Kimsey, Bucky	FB	200	5–11	So
Kitchens, Steve	LB	200	5–11	So
Lawrence, Kent	**TB**	**175**	**6–0**	**Sr**
Layfield, Jimmy	LG	220	5–11	Sr
Leath, Dennis	DB	190	5–11	So
Lopatka, Mike	LB	210	6–0	So
Lyons, Tommy	**C**	**210**	**6–2**	**So**
Marbury, Felix	DB	180	5–11	So
McConnell, Wayne	TE	215	6–2	So
McCullough, Jim	**PK**	**205**	**5–11**	**Jr**
McGill, Curtis	LT	230	6–4	Jr
McKibbon, Jeff	C	215	6–2	So
McKinnon, Bobby	DB	192	6–1	So
McKnight, David	**DE**	**182**	**6–1**	**Jr**
McPipkin, Paul	RG	210	6–2	So
Monk Bobby	RG	235	6–3	So
Montgomery, Jack	QB	190	6–0	So
Oakes, Mike	FB	185	5–10	So
Osbolt, Terry	DL	230	6–2	Sr

Player	Pos.	Wt.	Ht.	Yr.
Outlar, Barry	SE	175	5–10	So
Paine, Trav	WB	185	5–11	Jr
Payne Billy	**DE**	**205**	**6–1**	**Sr**
Pennington, Penny	**DB**	**175**	**5–9**	**Sr**
Rajecki, Peter	PK	180	5–9	Jr
Rholetter, David	**LT**	**240**	**6–2**	**Sr**
Robison, Dennard	DE	195	6–2	Jr
Rodrigue, Pat	**RG**	**215**	**5–11**	**Sr**
Rogers, Ronnie	LT	230	6–2	Jr
Russell, Phillip	DE	196	6–2	Jr
Satterwhite, Robert	RG	205	6–1	So
Saye, David	DT	220	6–2	So
Scott, Jake	**S**	**188**	**6–1**	**Jr**
Shaw, Ken	SE	183	6–2	So
Shirer, Jimmy	DB	180	5–11	So
Simpson, Robert	TE	205	6–3	So
Smaha, Jiggy	DT	230	6–3	Sr
Smiley, Julian	TB	203	6–0	So
Smith, Royce	RT	220	6–3	So
Stanfill, Bill	**DT**	**245**	**6–5**	**Sr**
Stewart, Mark	**DB**	**190**	**6–1**	**Sr**
Swindle, Buck	S	180	6–3	So
Tarrer, Harold	LB	210	6–2	Sr
Teel, Kerry	LB	200	5–11	So
Tucker, Mayo	DT	215	6–1	So
Watson, Dennis	DT	217	6–2	So
White, George	C	205	6–1	Sr
Whittemore, Charles	**SE**	**193**	**6–0**	**So**
Wood, Jimmy	DL	230	6–2	So
Woodall, Woody	PK–T	230	6–4	Jr
Woodward, Steve	WB	188	5–11	Sr
Yawn, Bruce	**LG**	**209**	**5–11**	**Sr**

1980
12–0–0
(includes 17–10 Sugar Bowl victory over Notre Dame
in national championship game)
Consensus national champions
Vince Dooley, *Head Coach*

Player	Pos.	Wt.	Ht.	Yr.
Arnold, Amp	**FL**	**170**	**6–0**	**Sr**
Ballard, Marty	OT	260	6–4	Sr
Bell, Greg	CB	185	5–11	Sr
Belue, Buck	**QB**	**185**	**6–1**	**Jr**
Blakewood, Jim	**LG**	**230**	**6–2**	**Jr**
Bobo, Tim	DE	205	6–2	So
Bouchillon, Keith	DE	206	6–2	Sr
Broadway, Jim	P	170	5–10	So
Brown, James	TE	217	6–3	So
Brown, Norris	**TE**	**215**	**6–3**	**So**
Buckler, Lon	FL	187	5–11	So
Campbell, Scott	G	235	6–4	So
Cannon, Keith	G	240	6–4	So
Carver, Dale	DE	215	6–2	So
Case, Tim	T	245	6–4	So
Charping, Stan	PK	190	5–9	So
Creamons, Joe	DL	240	6–2	Jr
Crowe, Tim	**DL**	**232**	**6–1**	**So**
Fisher, Mike	**CB**	**180**	**6–0**	**Sr**
Forts, Will	LB	205	6–0	So
Gargell, Guy	TE	215	6–0	So

Georgia National Champion Rosters

Player	Pos.	Wt.	Ht.	Yr.
Guthrie, Ed	FB	200	5–11	Sr
Hall, Keith	DE	190	6–1	Jr
Harper, Jeff	**LT**	**240**	**6–2**	**Sr**
Hipp, Jeff	**S**	**195**	**6–3**	**Sr**
Hudson, Nat	**RT**	**260**	**6–3**	**Sr**
Jackson, Kevin	DL	255	6–2	So
Junior, Charles	SE	178	6–0	So
Kelly, Bob	S	176	5–11	Sr
Kelly, Steve	TB	178	5–9	Jr
Kesler, George	C	205	6–1	Sr
Lamar, Frederick	LB	218	6–1	So
Lastinger, John	QB	190	6–2	So
Leusenring, Dan	C	248	6–2	So
Lindsey, Jack	DL	238	6–2	So
Lott, Jeff	CB	176	5–9	Jr
Malkiewicz, Mark	**P**	**203**	**6–2**	**Sr**
Malloy, Harold	T	245	6–5	So
Marlow, Dan	DE	215	6–3	So
Martin, Charles	DL	210	5–11	Fr
McCarthy, Chris	FB	202	5–11	So
McIntyre, Guy	T	235	6–3	So
McMickens, Donnie	TB	200	5–11	Sr
McShea, Pat	**DE**	**211**	**6–2**	**Sr**
Middleton, Keith	LB	217	6–1	Sr
Miles, Robert	**DE**	**225**	**6–4**	**Sr**
Miller, Mark	LB	201	6–0	Sr
Morrison, Tim	**RG**	**260**	**6–3**	**Sr**

BULLDOG MADNESS

Player	Pos.	Wt.	Ht.	Yr.
Mullis, Mitch	LB	205	5–10	So
Nall, Hugh	**C**	**235**	**6–0**	**Sr**
Nix, Tommy	C	200	6–1	Sr
Norris, Carnie	TB	190	5–9	So
Painter, David	SE	180	6–2	So
Parks, Tim	DL	245	6–3	Sr
Paulk, Jeff	ROV	190	6–1	So
Payne, Jimmy	**DT**	**243**	**6–4**	**So**
Radloff, Wayne	G	230	6–5	So
Robinson, Rex	**PK**	**215**	**6–0**	**Sr**
Ros, Frank	**LB**	**218**	**6–1**	**Sr**
Russell, Jay	FLK	171	5–11	Sr
Sawyer, Davy	QB	191	6–3	Jr
Scott, Lindsay	**SE**	**190**	**6–1**	**Jr**
Simon, Matt	TB	190	6–0	Jr
Singleton, Richard	ROV	200	6–0	So
Steber, Joel	C	226	6–0	So
Steel, Mike	G	229	6–2	So
Stewart, Ronnie	FB	202	5–10	Jr
Taylor, Nate	**LB**	**198**	**5–11**	**So**
Thompson, Mac	DT	250	6–6	So
Walker, Herschel	**TB**	**218**	**6–1**	**Fr**
Weaver, Eddie	**DL**	**270**	**6–0**	**Jr**
Welton, Chris	**ROV**	**200**	**6–1**	**Sr**
Williams, Dale	CB	168	6–0	Jr
Woerner, Scott	**CB**	**195**	**6–0**	**Sr**
Womack, Jimmy	**FB**	**200**	**5–9**	**Sr**
Young, Barry	FB	210	6–1	Fr

BIBLIOGRAPHY AND SOURCES

Adventure Quest, Inc. *The Heisman: Sixty Years of Tradition and Excellence.* Bronxville, N.Y.: Adventure Quest, Inc., 1995.

Bolton, Clyde. *Silver Britches.* West Point, N.Y.: Leisure Press, 1982.

Buchanan, Lamont. *The Story of Football.* New York: The Vanguard Press, Inc., 1952.

Claassen, Harold. *Football's Unforgettable Games.* New York: The Ronald Press Co., 1963.

Cromartie, Bill. *There Goes Herschel.* New York: Leisure Press, 1983.

Doherty, Terry. "Georgia's Quiet Man." *Daily News.* Sept. 9, 1988.

Dooley, Vince with Loran Smith. *Dooley's Dawgs: 25 Years of Winning Football at the University of Georgia.* Atlanta, Ga.: Longstreet Press, Inc., 1989.

Griffin, John Chandler. *Georgia vs. Georgia Tech: Gridiron Grudge since 1893.* Athens, Ga.: Hill Street Press, 2000.

Hundley, Jeff. "True Love." *Bulldog Magazine.* November 1989: 10, 11.

First Annual Peach Bowl Program—LSU vs. FSU. Atlanta, Ga.: General Lithographing Co., Dec. 30, 1968: 10.

Harper, Billy. "Hampton's in Same Class with Walker." *Athens Daily.* Nov. 2, 1989.

Klobuchar, Joe and Fran Tarkenton. *Tarkenton.* New York: Harper & Row, Publishers, 1976.

Knight Ridder Newspapers. "Georgia's Comeback Biggest Ever." *The (Nashville) Tennessean.* Jan. 2, 2000.

Leckie, Robert. *The Story of Football.* New York: Random House, Inc., 1965.

Little, Tom. *Bulldogs with a Bite.* Montgomery, Ala.: L&M Corp., 1966.

Martin, Charles E. *I've Seen 'Em All.* Athens, Ga.: Charles E. Martin, 1961.

Newberry, Paul. "Georgia's Edwards Hits Stride." *USA TODAY.* Nov. 13, 1997.

Outlar, Jesse. *Between the Hedges.* Huntsville, Ala.: The Strode Publishers, 1973.

Schlabach, Mark. "Edwards Makes Good on Second Chance." *Atlanta Journal-Constitution,* Nov. 15, 1997.

Scherer, George. *Auburn–Georgia Football—A Hundred Years of Rivalry.* Jefferson, N.C.: McFarland & Co., Inc., 1992.

Smith, Derek. *Glory Yards.* Nashville, Tenn.: Rutledge Hill Press, 1993.

Smith, Loran with Lewis Grizzard. *Glory! Glory!* Atlanta, Ga.: Peachtree Publishers Ltd., 1981.

Smith, Loran, ed. *Between the Hedges: 100 Years of Georgia Football.* Atlanta, Ga.: Longstreet Press, 1992.

Stegeman, John F. *The Ghosts of Herty Field: Early Days on a Southern Gridiron.* Athens, Ga.: University of Georgia Press, 1966.

Stern, Bill. *Bill Stern's Favorite Football Stories.* New York: Doubleday & Co., Inc., 1950.

Thilenius, Ed and Jim Koger. *No Ifs, No Ands, A Lot of . . . Butts.* Atlanta, Ga.: Foote and Davis, Inc., 1960.

Towers, Chip. "The Red Blur." *Athens Daily,* Aug. 19, 1995.

Towers, Chip. "Edwards: Take 2." *Athens Daily.* Aug. 25, 1996.

University of Georgia Athletic Association. *Georgia 1964.* Athens, Ga.: 1964.

University of Georgia Athletic Association. *Georgia 1966.* Athens: Ga.: 1966.

University of Georgia Athletic Association. *The 1998 University of Georgia Football Media Guide.* Athens, Ga: 1998.

University of Georgia Athletic Association. *The 2004 University of Georgia Football Media Guide.* Athens, Ga: 2004.

Vancil, Mark, ed. *ABC Sports College Football All-Time All-America Team.* New York: ABC Sports, Inc., 2000.

Whittingham, Richard. *Rites of Autumn: The Story of College Football.* New York: The Free Press, 2001.

WEB SITES:

http://georgiadogs.collegesports.com/sports/m-footbl/recaps/010105aaa.html

http://georgiadogs.collegesports.com/sports/mfootbl/mtt/richt_mark00.html

http://georgiadogs.collegesports.com/sports/m-footbl/specrel/120804aac.html

http://secsports.com/index.php?well_id=2&url_publish_channel_id=1915

http://66.102.7.104/search?q=cache:d1qRxGXxTDwJ:www.savannahmorningnews.com/stories/080201/SPTsecnote.shtml+Matt+Stinchcomb,+Georgia,+quotes&hl=en

http://www.mepuppy.com/articles/dogs-article–829.htm

http://www.cw.ua.edu/vnews/display.v/ART/2002/10/07/3da1060167f2c

http://albanyherald.net/sports archive/1202/sport120502.html

http://www.colts.com/sub.cfm?page=history_playerinfo&player_id=9

http://georgiadogs.collegesports.com/sports/m-footbl/specrel/051702aaa.html

http://p200.ezboard.com/fnfl-draftblitzfrm1.showMessage?topicID=2319.topic

http://www.redandblack.com/vnews/display.v/ART/2002/11/06/3dc91b0f8b0bd?in_archive=1

http://66.102.7.104/search?q=cache:QwAXPQ56VIJ:www.ajc.com/uga/content/sports/uga/dooley/+Bill+Stanfill,+quotes&hl=en

http://www.collegesports.com/tsx/current/m-footbl/geo.html#

http://64.233.179.104/search?q=cache:p-HWN7VfTdwJ:www.savannahmorningnews.com/stories/063004/2271507.shtml+2002+Georgia+Bulldogs,+quotes&hl=en

INDEX